*Management of Sites and
Services Housing Schemes*

Management of Sites and Services Housing Schemes

The Asian Experience

Peter J. Swan
Asian Institute of Technology, Bangkok

Emiel A. Wegelin
Institute for Housing Studies, Rotterdam

and

Komol Panchee
National Housing Authority, Bangkok

JOHN WILEY & SONS

Chichester · New York · Brisbane · Toronto · Singapore

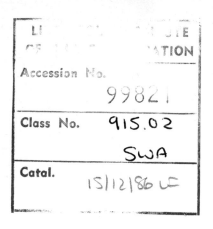
Library of Congress Cataloging in Publication Data:

Swan, Peter J.
 Management of sites and services housing schemes.

 Includes index.
 1. Public housing — Asia — Congresses. I. Wegelin, E. A.
II. Panchee, K. III. Title.
HD7288.78.A8W43 1983 363.5′8 82-13632

ISBN 0 471 90072 9 (cloth)
ISBN 0 471 90073 7 (paper)

British Library Cataloguing in Publication Data:

Management of sites and services housing schemes:
 the Asian experience.
 1. Public housing — Asia — Congresses
 2. Housing management — Asia — Congresses
I. Swan, P. J. II. Wegelin, E. A.
III. Panchee, K.
363.5′8′068 TX960

ISBN 0 471 90072 9 (cloth)
ISBN 0 471 90073 7 (paper)

Phototypeset by Dobbie Typesetting Service, Plymouth, Devon.
Printed by the Pitman Press Ltd., Bath, Avon.

Contents

Preface

An international seminar with the title 'Sites and Services Schemes: Exploring the Asian Experience' was held in Bangkok during 5–16 January 1981. At the seminar 14 project experiences from five different Asian countries were discussed by project managers, architects, planners, and other professionals involved in the planning and/or implementation of these projects. Sharing these project experiences was complemented by references to similar experience in Africa and Latin America, while the participants in the seminar also benefited from a reflection on the World Bank's experience in funding sites and services projects.

As the material presented by the participants at the seminar comprised such a unique collection of Asian project data we felt that it would be useful to make it available to a wider audience. Reactions to the book from independent reviewers have reinforced our own view that this material represents an instructive text for training courses, for students and practitioners of housing administration, planning and architecture not only in Asia but throughout the Third World. We hope that the book will be of use to both practitioners and academics in the quest further to refine the sites and services strategy, which turns out to be a much more complex process than was originally thought.

In order to make the material more easily accessible, the book is organized in accordance with a project development sequence, moving from concepts through planning and implementation to estate management and community development issues. In doing so, the main text of the book draws heavily on common experiences and problems expressed by the seminar participants. This sequence facilitates its use as a manual. Specific issues dealt with in each chapter are illustrated with detailed case studies of the best documented projects presented at the seminar, supplemented where possible with more recent data obtained by the authors.

As is clear from the above, this book focuses on the implementation experience with the sites and services housing approach in Asia. This is only one of the low income housing approaches recently adopted in Third World countries within the framework of new and more appropriate low income housing policies. Some of the salient policy issues are touched upon in this book, but for a more wide-ranging review of low income housing policies the reader is referred to the companion volume to this book, edited by Geoffrey Payne, entitled *Low Income Housing in Developing Countries.*

x

The authors are indebted to many institutions and individuals. The seminar in part and the preparation of the book were funded by the Netherlands government through the Institute for Housing Studies' support of the Training Centre for Urban Low-income Housing Development at the National Housing Authority of Thailand. Participants in the seminar presented a rich project database which was essential in developing the book in its present shape. The help of Mr Pichai Intarachai in preparing the drawings and maps and of Miss Kamolwan Thongsuk in typing the various versions of the manuscript is gratefully acknowledged. The interpretations and conclusions we have drawn from the seminar of course are our own, and do not necessarily reflect the views of the sponsors or participants.

PETER J. SWAN, KOMOL PANCHEE
and EMIEL A. WEGELIN

Bangkok,
June 1982

List of Participants

Name	Position/Organization	Project/City/Country
Mr Angelito S. Lazaro	Project Manager/ National Housing Authority	Dasmariñas/Quezon City/ Philippines
Mr Andres C. Lingan	Project Superintendent/ National Housing Authority	Dasmariñas/Quezon City/ Philippines
Mrs Zonia Galvez	Architect Planner/ National Housing Authority	Dagat-Dagatan/Manila/ Philippines
Mr Narciso C. Adaya	Project Manager/ National Housing Authority	Dagat-Dagatan/Manila/ Philippines
Mr Mohammad I. Mirza	Deputy Director, Karachi Development Authority	Metroville Settlement Programme/Karachi/Pakistan
Mr. A. R. Khan	Superintending Engineer, Karachi Development Authority	Metroville Settlement Programme/Karachi/Pakistan
Mr R. Setiadjid Imam	Project Manager, Perumnas	Simomulyo/Surabaya/ Indonesia
Mr Saleh	Head of Survey Section/ Directorate of Building Research	Bekasi/Jakarta/Indonesia
Mr Moh Besar	Project Manager, Perumnas	Bekasi/Jakarta/Indonesia
Mr Ario Rachmadi	Architect, Directorate of Housing	Medan sites and services/ Medan Indonesia
Mr Budi Prabowo	Project Manager, Perumnas	Medan sites and services/ Medan Indonesia
Mr Vijay D. Risbud	Dy. Director/Delhi Development Authority	Dakschinpuri/New Delhi/ India
Mr Harish C. Gupta	Executive Engineer/ Delhi Development Authority	Dakschinpuri/New Delhi/ India

Name	Position/Organization	Project/City/Country
Mr Pratul K. Dutta	Director of Planning/ Calcutta Metropolitan Development Authority	Baishnavghata-Patuli/ Calcutta/India
Mr Bibhas Chatterjee	Deputy Secretary, Estate Management	Baishnavghata-Patuli/ Calcutta/India
Mr S. P. Kumaresan	Superintending Engineer, Tamil Nadu Housing Board	Arumbakkam/Madras/ India
Mr A. Lakshmanan	Senior Deputy Planner, Madras Metropolitan Development Authority	Arumbakkam/Madras/ India
Mr Rupesh Jaiswal	Executive Engineer, Kanpur Development Authority	Kanpur Urban Project/ Kanpur/India
Mr B. N. Singh	Senior Planner, Government of Uttar Pradesh	Kanpur Urban Project/ Kanpur/India
Mr M. Y. Thackerey	Chief Architect, City and Industrial Development Corporation	Vashi/Bombay/India
Mr D. G. Parab	Senior Planner, City and Industrial Development Corporation	Vashi/Bombay/India
Mr Tospol Chantarawong	Chief of Project & Planning National Housing Authority Section	Bang Plee/Bangkok/ Thailand
Mr Aran Karukose	Architect/National Housing Authority	Bang Plee/Bangkok/ Thailand
Mr Suthep Chaimungkalanon	Architect/National Housing Authority	Bang Plee/Bangkok/ Thailand
Mr Seri Kirisri	Head of Financial Policy Section/National Housing Authority	Tung Song Hong/Bangkok/ Thailand
Mr Prakit Tancharoen	Engineer/National Housing Authority	Tung Song Hong/Bangkok/ Thailand
Mr Pramode Chaipoon	Architect/National Housing Authority	Tung Song Hong/Bangkok/ Thailand
Mr Komson Suksumake	Architect/National Housing Authority	Rangsit/Bangkok/ Thailand
Mr Somsak Nakngeonthong	Head of Rangsit Area Office/National Housing Authority	Rangsit/Bangkok/ Thailand

Chapter 1

Understanding the Sites and Services Housing Strategy

1.1 Introduction

Recent attempts at unconventional and innovative approaches to low income housing like sites and services have evolved from a very down to earth review of what housing really is and what it had always been in the centuries prior to industrialization and the advent of government housing agencies. This rediscovery of how ordinary people traditionally obtain shelter came at a time when a dilemma in housing activity by government agencies was being confronted. In the process of trying to improve the housing conditions of the urban poor, such agencies were bankrupting themselves in building far too few, far too expensive housing units and, at the same time, were destroying the existing housing stock of a large number of poor urban families because they were illegal. These houses were considered illegal because they were on land that did not belong to the occupants and because they were not up to the high structural standards dictated by the urban building codes which, in many cases, were a colonial heritage from developed countries. The net effect, year by year, was to dehouse a growing number of urban poor.

Thus, instead of improving the habitat of large numbers of urban poor, conventional housing programmes were often providing small numbers of families with expensive, subsidized housing (usually in the form of high-rise flats) but demolishing, in much greater quantities, the housing stock that the poor had organized for themselves at no direct cost to government agencies. Furthermore, this informal sector housing of slum and squatter communities was affordable to low income families and was usually a better arrangement in terms of location and employment opportunities. Over the last decade a growing number of professionals in the low income housing field have pointed out that the supply of housing at costs commensurate with income was generally lagging behind needs because resources were either insufficient or not effectively mobilized. One of the major resources, they noted, that was not even recognized was the investment of labour and materials by the poor in the housing stock they produced themselves. Conventional housing projects, on the other hand, were generally found to be neither socially appropriate nor

1

economically viable,* new strategies had to be found which could reduce the economic and administrative burdens of housing agencies and could mobilize the resources of the target groups.

Much of the pressure to review the role of government housing agencies following the renewed recognition of the informal housing efforts of the poor themselves has come from international agencies rather than from national or local governments. The logic was simple but persuasive. Government agencies were not able to produce sufficient housing units at costs which the poor could afford. The poor had been able to fend better on their own. Would not a supportive and facilitating role by government agencies be more appropriate to augment this supply of housing stock, through delivering land, utilities and services to poor households unable to acquire these themselves? Two strategies that sprang from this line of reasoning were to improve the environment and access to utilities in existing settlements and to open up serviced plots of land in planned sites on which people could gradually develop their own housing. The former strategy is slum improvement or slum upgrading and the latter is called sites and services.

Without doubt the major promoter of slum improvement and sites and services schemes is the International Bank for Reconstruction and Development (World Bank). In a 1974 World Bank paper — 'Sites and Services Projects' — it was argued that sites and services projects and slum improvement programmes were complementary strategies that held out considerable hope of overcoming pressing needs in low income urban housing.

> In these circumstances, the provision of new tracts of urbanized land in convenient locations with the basic supporting services needed to produce viable low income communities, can present many advantages and yet fall within both general resource availabilities and the ability of recipients to pay. Such 'sites and services' projects can provide:
>
> — a greatly increased supply of building plots with urban infrastructure and services that, while economical of resources, cannot be readily supplied on an unorganized basis;
> — efficient new townships with more efficient urban development patterns;
> — much better physical living conditions than are available in unplanned squatter settlements;
> — increased scope for self help construction providing dwellings at minimum cost while stimulating non-monetary savings and income;
> — significantly improved employment opportunities and training;

---

* Exceptions in Asia are Singapore, Hong Kong and, to a lesser extent, Malaysia and South Korea. For a detailed social cost-benefit analysis of six conventional projects in Malaysia, see Wegelin (1978).

— security of tenure and a basis for community development;
— a better general environment.

Upgrading schemes to improve conditions in existing squatter settlements through the provision of public utilities and community services can, under appropriate conditions, secure similar benefits. (International Bank for Reconstruction and Development, 1974, p.2).

It is important from the outset to understand that sites and services projects are not comprehensive solutions but rather a significant component in a larger planning strategy. That strategy envisages the government's role in services supply and planning matters as well as the provision of land and the creation of supportive financial, administrative and legal contexts in which local communities can function. It is also clear that sites and services schemes cannot be expected to cater for the lowest income groups whose precarious livelihoods render them extremely weak economically and inflexible in terms of location. The slum improvement schemes are more specifically directed to these very low income groups.

Sites and services are addressed to a fairly large middle stratum of the low income groups to meet enormous and growing backlogs of services, utilities and shelter at comparatively low costs and on a realistic scale. Sites and services projects mean making available serviced building plots, possibly with core or fully built housing in urban (usually peripheral) locations. In practice these projects usually entail many of the following activities: land selection and acquisition, site design and preparation, selection of appropriate residents, core house construction, the supply of utilities and community services, estate management, payment collection and, often, the setting up of community organizations.

Other goals implicit in the sites and services strategy are to allow planners to gain some control over national urban growth patterns and to reduce one of the biggest obstacles to low income housing, namely land speculation. Naturally, it was hoped that if far-sighted and public-spirited politicians and government officials could take up large tracts of land on city and town peripheries well before natural city growth had begun to inflate the prices, then, not only could plot costs for incoming low income communities be kept low, but the increased availability of home plots in the city as a whole could help restrain land prices in intermediate urban areas. However, no clear mechanism for doing this has yet been identified in most Asian urban contexts. In some cities in Pakistan and India, where governments already hold such tracts of land, it has been found that such public ownership of land has not been sufficient to curb land speculation.

1.2 Self Help and Community Participation in Sites and Services

Perhaps the most significant feature of the sites and services approach is its primary reliance on community participation in the planning of the project as well as in the building, improvement, maintenance and management thereof. It is certainly the component that has been most misunderstood by the World Bank itself and by project implementing government housing agencies. Although people's participation in planning is almost invariably discussed and applauded in project proposals, it has seldom been sought in practice. Usually the only form of participation actually encouraged, though often highly regulated, is in terms of labour for construction.

The obstacles to understanding the approach and being able to design and implement sites and services projects successfully mainly stem from the attitudes and perceptions of roles of politicians, government bureaucrats and housing professionals. They have become accustomed to seeing low income housing and urban planning as their business. They plan and coordinate the growth of cities and they control the standards of formal (i.e. legal) housing. In another sense, they see a role for themselves as benefactors of the under-privileged and in this capacity they try to deliver housing to various deserving target groups. It is, therefore, hard for them to turn around and accept that 90 per cent or more of low income people actually do manage some kind of housing arrangement without assistance. It is even harder for them to move from such an acceptance to the further understanding that the most effective thing they can do is simply to create access to improved housing contexts and let the poor legally continue to take responsibility for the provision, improvement and maintenance of their own shelter. There is a natural aversion to handing over such responsibility and autonomy to the people because, in terms of their traditional bureaucratic role, bureaucrats and professionals fear being rendered redundant.

In fact, this perception is incorrect as there is an important role for housing bureaucrats and professionals to play in terms of planning for and supporting the private efforts of the poor in housing and infrastructural improvement. The urban systems in which such low income housing activity is taking place are in considerable physical, economic and social disarray. The fundamental issue is, of course, land, and it is around this question that so much work in terms of research, innovation and control needs to be done, perhaps primarily by government agencies. There are other issues too, that relate to the availability and suitability of community organizations, of building materials, of building and design skills, of finance and of public urban priorities in general.

Sites and services projects have to be implemented in complex economic, social and political environments. The planners, architects and other housing professionals are forced to come out into a real physical and social class environment in which they often feel uncomfortable and possibly threatened because, instead of dealing with powerless and passive individual families, they are expected to support active and potentially powerful communities. The bureaucratic and professional preoccupation with control through endless procedure is not appropriate in this scenario. The whole key to success is to win the confidence of the sites and services participants and to maximize the value of self help which, in turn, means allowing them to take the initiative of self-management whenever possible.

1.3 The Asian Experience

Experimenting with sites and services is a challenge to politicians and housing agencies. It involves complex analysis and planning. The time frames of sites and services projects are lengthy — usually a minimum of 5 to 6 years from the first planning stages through to completion. Furthermore, as housing projects they are novel and unfamiliar to the general public and to the target groups themselves and hence provoke mixed responses, sometimes controversy and recrimination. Therefore, it is surprising that so many countries in Asia (of widely differing political creeds) continue to experiment with such approaches, even without the incentives of huge loans from international agencies.

One general trend is clear. The more conservative and unresponsive the governments and government agencies are to the needs of the poor, the more plush and complete are the sites and services projects — more expensive infrastructure, more completely built units with higher construction standards, and less self-reliant but wealthier 'low income' clients. The more enterprising and responsive the government is to the needs of the poor, the more basic and transitional are the sites and services projects. In the former contexts the preoccupation of politicians and officials is to have a project site with sufficient cosmetic attraction to serve as an advertisement for their achievements. (This, too, is no doubt the case with high-rise flats and other government conventional housing construction.) In the latter cases the politicians must take satisfaction in having created housing opportunities for much larger numbers of families at a fraction of the cost to the nation at large. Though the settlements may be raw and untidy for a time, they will eventually mature into strong, self-reliant and diversified neighbourhoods.

The sites and services strategy as we find it in the following chapters is not a perfected approach because the contexts in which it is applied are conditioned by wider economic, political and social factors, and because varying contexts necessitate or enable specific experiments with particular project components. Some projects rely on existing city infrastructure networks, others have had to develop their own on site. Some projects resettle identified target groups or existing communities, others address themselves to broad low income ranges on a city-wide basis. Some involve several agencies in their design and implementation, others rely only on one agency. Such factors limit the scope for a rigid project comparison or for a conclusive evaluation of the relevance and effectiveness of the strategy *per se* for Asian cities.

Nevertheless, the projects discussed in this book provide useful insights into the processes of planning and implementation as well as some feedback on how acceptable projects are to the target groups themselves. Furthermore, there are signs that sites and services projects are evolving into more appropriate forms, in accordance with the development of more experienced and enthusiastic agencies.

1.4 Case Study Focus

The first phase of the first case study, the Dagat-Dagatan sites and services project, was initially undertaken by the National Housing Authority of the Philippines in response to the need for an overspill area for its Tondo Foreshore slum improvement project. In subsequent phases the project matured into a more realistic sites and services scheme in its own right. It is a huge undertaking that seeks to benefit more than 15,000 families over a period of over 6 years. It is centrally located and will accommodate families of income levels ranging from the 10th to the 65th percentiles of the urban household income distribution. It has been planned with a clear perception of the need to relate housing arrangements to employment opportunities. It is an appropriate introductory case through which one can identify the diversity of issues involved in designing and implementing large-scale sites and services projects.

Case Study I DAGAT-DAGATAN SITES AND SERVICES PROJECT, MANILA

(I) Urban Context

Approximately 30 per cent of the Philippine urban population is estimated to be living at or below the minimum subsistence level without adequate housing and limited access to water, sanitary facilities and electricity.* While the proportion of urban poor in Metropolitan Manila is about the same as in other major cities, the poor of Metro Manila constitute the largest single concentration of poverty in the country, totalling 1.5 million or nearly 50 per cent of the national total. Some 34 per cent of Metro Manila families in 1971 had incomes below the Food Threshold, and 52 to 59 per cent had incomes below the Total Threshold.† Additionally, Metro Manila has an unemployment rate of 11 per cent compared with 7 per cent nationally.

In January 1981, the Metropolitan Manila Area had an estimated population

---

* The minimum subsistence level is defined by FAO/WHO as the ability to afford a minimum adequate diet.
† Government of the Philippines, '1976 Philippine Poverty Thresholds'. The Food Threshold is based on the Food and Nutrition Research Council of the Philippines' calculated nutritionally adequate minimum-cost diet. The food budget, when spent on the recommended amount of food, is able to satisfy the requirements to sustain life and maintain an individual for productive work. The total Threshold is substantially based on a method of the US Social Security Administration which calls for the application of a multiplier to a nutritionally adequate diet. The multiplier is the reciprocal of an 'ideal' proportion of food expenditures to the total budget.

of 7 million or 14.6 per cent of the national total.* With an average growth rate of 5 per cent since 1960 Manila's population is increasing faster than those of other urban areas because of higher rates of migration to Manila.

The city's most pressing problems relate to shelter, health and malnutrition, urban transport and institutional capabilities. About 1.3 million currently live in substandard structures on unserviced lots with very low levels of environmental sanitation. The inadequacy of sanitation facilities (compounded by flooding) and of health services has led to a deterioration in the level of health.

An acute housing shortage has been caused by rapid population growth, inadequate housing stock, rampant land speculation and the absence of finance mechanisms to assist low income families in their housing efforts. In 1975 the National Housing Authority (NHA) was created to centralize the six agencies formerly concerned with the provision of housing in order to set about meeting the escalating requirements for better shelter in the Philippines. A variety of programmes have been formulated and are currently being implemented, including large-scale slum upgrading programmes and sites and services projects.

(II) Target Population

The Dagat-Dagatan sites and services project is designed to benefit three groups. The first priority families are those that are to be relocated from Tondo Foreshore nearby and the Dagat-Dagatan area itself. Second priority is being given to those households that require relocation from slum improvement projects and to low income overspill population from the surrounding cities and municipalities. Third priority is being given to the lower income residents of Metro Manila as a whole.

The salient characteristics of this 'target' population have been studied in an effort to design the project according to their needs. The demographic evaluation of the target population considered the total and household population in six selected areas, namely Tondo Foreshore, International Port, Dagat-Dagatan, Navotas, Malabon, and Caloocan City (see location map). Growth estimates of the number of households in the target areas ranged from 4 to 9 per cent per annum within the period 1970 to 1975.

Population and household densities are relatively high with the exception of Dagat-Dagatan itself. Population densities are exceptionally high for Tondo Foreshore (981 persons per hectare) and International Port (654 persons per hectare). Likewise, highest household densities are found in Tondo Foreshore (161 households per hectare) and International Port (117 households per hectare). The average household consists of six persons and more than 60 per cent of these households are composed of nuclear families.

---

* Estimated from the 1980 census by the National Census and Statistical Office of the Philippines.

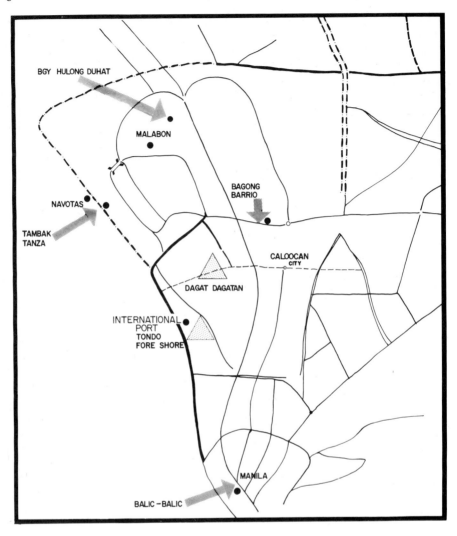

URBAN AREA AFFECTED

Location map: Dagat-Dagatan project, Manila

The target population is characteristically young with a predominance of females and correspondingly high fertility rates. The mean age is estimated to be 20 years and the median age is 17 years. About 50 per cent of females are of child bearing age. The target population is also characterized as having a high nuptiality level. This obviously contributes to sustained fertility.

The educational attainment level of the target population is relatively low. Almost 50 per cent have attained an elementary education, roughly 25 to 30 per cent have reached the secondary level and less than 10 per cent have reached the tertiary level.

Rural-urban migrants do not constitute a substantial portion of the target population in the selected areas. Tondo's population in 1970 was composed of 25 per cent migrants. Of those residing in the selected areas, only Malabon experienced a high level (20.1 per cent) of in-migration according to the 1975 census.

The working population of Dagat-Dagatan and Tondo Foreshore is mostly made up of unskilled and semi-skilled workers. The unskilled workers comprise 48 per cent of the total number employed, and 37 per cent of the workers and semi-skilled. The fisherman in Navotas and Dagat-Dagatan, who belong to a separate skills category, form the third largest grouping of skills in their respective areas. Nearly one person out of four in Navotas has skills related to fishing.

Very few are in occupations requiring high levels of skill. The distribution of occupants tends to indicate that vending is by far the largest occupational activity of the residents of the squatter areas. This reflects the number of persons who are working proprietors involved in small-scale merchandising. Other occupations exhibiting a concentration of workers are the crafts, service, sports, transport and communication sectors. The latter group of occupations is more evident in the Tondo Foreshore area, where many occupations such as those of stevedores and freight handlers are directly related to the activities of the nearby port.

Wage and salary workers comprise a very large percentage of the total number employed. In squatter areas over 58 per cent of full-time workers are either private or government employees. The number of self-employed is considerable and may be seen as an adaptive response to the earning opportunities in the community. A large number of workers are paid on a commission or piece rate basis so their incomes vary with the volume of their output.

Extensive research indicated that to cater for the primary target population, the housing opportunities of Dagat-Dagatan had to be designed to be affordable by Metro Manila households below the 65th percentile in the Metro Manila income distribution.

(III) Land Selection and Acquisition

The 435 hectare site was by far the largest undeveloped area within Metro Manila. The project land was formerly privately owned and was comprised of fish ponds. Industrial development along the periphery had resulted in serious pollution of these ponds, rendering the original land use unprofitable. The site was expropriated by the NHA in 1975 and has been reclaimed by the Ministry of Public Works in phases.

As reclaimed land it has proved to be relatively cheap in comparison with other parcels in similar locations. As such it provides a unique opportunity within inner Metro Manila to provide housing opportunities for the lowest income groups. The location of the site in relation to the port and to three primary transportation routes enhances the possibility of establishing an export-oriented, labour-intensive commercial and industrial area in Dagat-Dagatan which would provide a solid economic base for the target population.

(IV) Actors in Project Design and Implementation

The National Housing Authority executes the Dagat-Dagatan project under the direct management of the Dagat-Dagatan Project Office. The organizational structure for the Dagat-Dagatan Project Office includes divisions of Planning, Construction, Estate Management, Community Development, Livelihood Development, Finance and Administration. The heads of these divisions are responsible for the execution of work in their particular units under the supervision and control of the project manager.

The chief engineer heads the Construction Division. He directs and supervises closely the implementation/construction management of the project with the concurrence of the project manager. He is being assisted by the project engineers and inspectors as well as foreign and local consultants. Such a system of management is considered to be working well. Policy matters that are not within the authority of the project manager and/or chief engineer are decided by the general manager of the National Housing Authority. The project is partly financed by the World Bank, therefore any proposed deviation from agreed standards or arrangements has to be forwarded to and approved by the World Bank.

The community is active in community meetings, mostly in the planning stage of on-plot provision and in community development programmes. Its opinions and recommendations have been influential in the formulation of plans and programmes. The Community Development Division has constant dialogues with various community organizations for a continuous review of technical options and proposals.

The project is being developed in nine phases. The first phase was completed in 1978 under the Tondo Foreshore development project.* The subsequent eight phases are being implemented by the Dagat-Dagatan Project Office. The two basic elements involved are major infrastructural works and subdivisions land development. The Barangay units (neighbourhood clusters) are the basic elements in phasing residential development. Community facilities for each residential area are built so as to be operational when the allottees take up ther plots.

In order to ascertain timely completion and conformity to plans and specifications, a weekly conference with contractors is held to discuss problems and issues affecting the project. In addition, daily project reports are consolidated for incorporation in a quarterly report for evaluation and assessment by higher authorities including the World Bank.

---

* This project is essentially a slum upgrading project that involved reblocking the slum housing stock. The process of reblocking is such that not all households could be retained in the Tondo Foreshore area. Such 'overspill' households have been rehoused in Dagat-Dagatan phase I, approximately 4 kilometres from Tondo.

(V) Site Planning and Infrastructural Development

The principal constraint to development was the lack of major infrastructure to serve the site and its environs. The technical problem of draining the site as well as the adjacent residential areas affected by the reclamation scheme necessitated the improvement of several existing waterways and the construction of new facilities. The total area reclaimed amounted to 377.50 hectares.

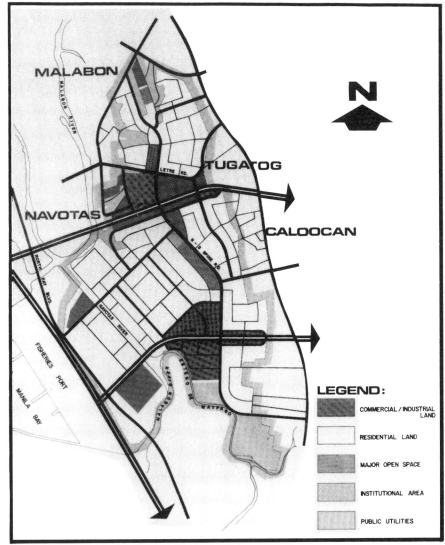

TOTAL AREA IN HECTARES: 377.5
TOTAL OF DWELLINGS/PLOTS: 18,000

TOTAL POPULATION: 200,000

Site plan: Dagat-Dagatan, Manila

The infrastructural components of the Dagat-Dagatan project — consisting of transportation/circulation, storm drainage, water supply and sewerage — are key elements affecting the implementation and success of the project. Implementation approaches for these components were selected from studies of several alternatives. A balance was sought for each component between standards or level of service, cost, and environmental effects.

The site roads are designed within the framework established by the three major roads servicing the site from other parts of Metro Manila (see site plan). A hierarchical road system has been developed to provide a variety of levels of service whilst limiting traffic passing through residential areas. A major road forms the main north–south spine between the two main east–west roads and serves as a major route for public transport and jeepneys (minibuses). Initially only one of the two carriageways is to be constructed. Secondary roads serve as public transportation and jeepney routes within the community.

The roads, the residential areas and community facilities are interconnected by a footpath system which serves as emergency access, fire breaks and servicing easements as well as circulation spaces. In terms of land use, circulation accounts for 10.3 per cent (39 hectares) of the total site (see Table 6, p.67).

It was necessary to provide the residents as well as the commercial and industrial installations which are being developed at Dagat-Dagatan, and the residents in adjacent areas, with a reasonable level of protection from the risk of flooding. This means that adequate temporary works had to be provided during ongoing reclamation phases. An acceptable standard of drainage had to be provided for residential and non-residential use which could still permit the upgrading of the existing inadequate drainage systems in adjacent areas without causing subsequent flooding in the Dagat-Dagatan site. On-site drainage (of developed areas) consists of surface drainage and pipes.

Off-site, substantial dredging was necessary to lower the water level in the regional river system. This work was carried out by the Department of Public Works, Transportation and Communications. Interceptor channels are currently being constructed by the NHA on site to cater for drainage from adjacent areas as well as from within the project area itself.

The water supply system is being developed within the overall framework of the Metropolitan Water Works and Sewerage System (MWSS). The MWSS is currently involved in a major upgrading of the system in the area of Dagat-Dagatan, including a major primary ring main, which will circumvent the site. Upon the completion of this in 1982, the entire developed site is expected to be adequately supplied with water of good quality.

In the interim a series of deep wells with on-site storage and pumping facilities are being constructed to meet the increasing site demand. This temporary water supply facility is designed and constructed by the NHA. It is expected that by the end of 1982 it will be redundant, because the distribution lines will be hooked up to the permanent water supply. Water in both the interim phase and in the permanent scheme is supplied to taps on each plot unit.

The system of sewage treatment developed for Dagat-Dagatan includes sewage collection, servicing individual allotments and a treatment facility consisting of aeration lagoons, polishing ponds and chlorination plants. The capacity of the plant will be increased by phases ultimately to service the entire Dagat-Dagatan area with its eventual population of 200,000. This facility is for interim use until the MWSS has developed its collective system in the area.

Electricity supply for the project is provided by the Manila Electric Company (MERALCO). Most of the primary poles are situated on perimeter streets at an average spacing of 50 metres. Secondary poles are located on interior streets at an average spacing of 35 metres. Natural wood poles treated with creosote are being used on both primary and secondary networks systems to minimize construction costs. Transformers are mounted on primary poles while street lights are on either primary or secondary poles. The service drop (of up to 30 metres), giving plot units individual connections, is supplied by the company. The power consumption by the individual resident families in this project is being measured by means of meters on an individual or group basis. A fixed rate has been set by MERALCO for consumers using minimal amounts of energy.

All told, utilities account for 9.21 per cent (34.75 hectares) of the total project site. Land for industrial and commercial use totals 75.5 hectares or 20.00 per cent of the site. Institutional land amounts to 6.5 hectares (1.72 per cent); open spaces amount to 7.75 hectares (2.15 per cent); and 214 hectares (56.68 per cent) is for residential use (see Table 6, p.67).

(VI) Industrial and Commercial Development, Income Generation, and Social Services

A principal planning requirement was the location of sufficient commercial and industrial areas to provide employment opportunities and cross-subsidy support for the housing areas. The cross-subsidy is necessary in order to reach the full range of income levels, especially the lowest percentiles, in the target group. The surplus from the sale of commercial and industrial zone land at market prices should generate the necessary resources to subsidize the sale of plots to lower income families.

As a resettlement site Dagat-Dagatan is exempt from the ban on certain industries within 50 kilometres of Metro Manila. Industrial and commercial areas are being developed and serviced as part of the project. An aggressive and innovative market strategy was perceived to be an essential determinant of their financial viability.

Manufactures are given various incentives by the NHA, including long-term and short-term credit assistance. The availability of manpower from amongst the residents within the project ensures a continuous flow of operations for these industries. The locational advantage of being within the Metropolitan Manila area, and having proximity to the central business district and the port, reduces transportation costs for these entrepreneurs.

As of September 1981, most industrial and commercial lots in phase I have already been applied for and awarded to a number of manufacturers/retailers (i.e. garment industries, steelworks, footwear shops, drugstore, etc.). Delay in the earthwork and roads leading to and from the second phase of industrial and commercial development has caused a slow uptake of these areas.

Income generating activities are being carried out by the Livelihood Development Division of the Project Office. These are subcontract brokeraging, such as job orders for tray straw embroidery, shellcraft, etc., which are offered to interested low income residents. Credit assistance is also being extended to entrepreneurs through the small business loan programmes, as well as technical assistance in terms of simple bookkeeping, cash flow analysis, market tie-up, and skills training to augment the residents' skills. These programmes are working fairly well. A livelihood interagency committee is being formed to strengthen the thrust of the income generating activities. Government agencies engaged in entrepreneurial and handicraft promotion activities are being utilized as well as local lending agencies.

In response to the needs of the target population, a full range of community facilities is being developed at Dagat-Dagatan. These facilities are not only intended to cater for the beneficiaries but also to alleviate some of the existing deficiencies in areas adjacent to the site.

Six new elementary schools, two new high schools and a reserved site for higher education are proposed to absorb a rapidly growing school population. Vocational training programmes are to be geared towards cultivating vocational skills among the young. Five health centres of various types and a reserve site for a 200-bed hospital will cater for the medical, maternal and child care needs of the area. Some 15 multipurpose neighbourhood centres (Barangay Day-Care Centres) are planned to provide a number of services and facilities at the local level. Besides providing day-care services, supplementary feeding for children aged from 3 to 6, handicraft training and nutritional workshops, these centres would also serve as recreational facilities and local meeting centres.

The community residents take responsibility for the collection and transfer of garbage from the housing cluster to points of collection along local collection roads. The collection from the storage bins provided is the responsibility of the Metro Manila Commission.

A site for a police precinct and fire station is available along the north–south spine of the project site.

(VII) Financial Arrangements

The financial objectives of the project are related to affordability, cost effectiveness and financial viability. The components of the project, particularly the housing opportunities, are designed and priced in such a way as to ensure that they are affordable by the target group. As the project strives to achieve full recovery of project costs in order to demonstrate the long-term replicability of a sites and services programme, it must be cost efficient in terms of design, layout and standards.

The project is being financed from a government loan, line agency contributions, and a loan from the International Bank for Reconstruction and Development. The development schedule was drawn up to achieve a rapid build-up of housing plots as well as an early inflow of revenues to the project from the sale of commercial/industrial land.

Total project costs include works both within and external to the site which will not be recovered from beneficiaries but which will be funded by various line agencies as grants. Cost allocation is generally based on the proportion of net land area devoted to each major land use. The total cost allocated to residential use is distributed to individual plots of the basis of an average cost per square metre for land, land reclamation, and infrastructure together with a specific charge for on-plot development options.

(VIII) Plot and Dwelling Options

Plots are allotted on a 25-year lease with an option for outright purchase or hire purchase. Full tenure is considered to be an important incentive for families to mobilize their savings and other resources to develop their units.

The programme of plot sizes, percentage distribution and on-plot options for Dagat-Dagatan has been shaped by various studies, including recent in-house NHA survey work.

First estimates of plot sizing and percentage distribution were made in the 'Consultants' Interim Report' (1977)* which quoted a Tondo Foreshore survey as revealing no correlation between plot size and its occupancy. The report predicted an average occupancy of about 10.4 persons per plot and proposed a range of plot sizes from 50 to 200 m^2. This provision has since been refined broadly to conform to a preferred IBRD range and distribution: i.e. 48 m^2— 12 per cent, 60 m^2—40 per cent, 72 m^2—20 per cent, 84 m^2—10 per cent, 98 m^2—10 per cent, 112-120 m^2—8 per cent, 120-150 m^2—2 per cent. It can be seen that the majority of plots (52 per cent) lie at the lower end of the range, but still allow satisfactory dwellings to be planned with adequate cross ventilation and fire protection. Minimum plot sizes are somewhat larger than those provided in the Tondo Foreshore development project, where dwelling development proved difficult in the 38–50 m^2 zone. The format of Dagat-Dagatan plots is limited to proportions of 1 : 1.7–2.7 to minimize frontages and consequently reduce infrastructure costs. The general percentage distribution of plots has been maintained without major changes through detailed planning (1978–1980).

However, considerable development has taken place in the design and distribution of on-plot provision. On-plot options in phase I (1,580 plots) and

* Llewelyn-Davies Kinhill Pty Ltd., with Sy Cip Corres Velayo & Co. The Second Feasibility Study in Dagat-Dagatan and Regional Centers, April 1977.

the earlier part of phase II were derived directly from the 'Consultants' Feasibility Report' (1978),* but it gradually became clear to the project management and to the IBRD that these options were proving too costly compared with realistic amortization payments. Substantial reductions both in the options themselves and in their number were necessary. An in-house study of September 1980, based on discussions with community representatives and earlier interviews with phase I residents, was undertaken with three objectives:

1 Control of project costs relative to price escalation of materials and labour.
2 Investigation of alternative on-plot development design that reflects the population's affordability levels.
3 Relevance of on-plot options and their respective advantages from the viewpoint of the beneficiaries.

Independent analysis suggested that the relevant options would have to cost no more than 50 per cent, typically, of those originally built. The in-house study concluded that:

1 On-plot development should only be provided for the smaller plots (50–84 m^2).
2 The basic minimum was adequate—sanitary core was the most useful option, provided that it was supported by the option of an NHA Home Materials Loan package, to allow beneficiaries to build from this core.
3 Early lot assignment was critical to give beneficiaries 1–2 months of construction time before actual relocation took place. A prerequisite for the

Dagat-Dagatan, phase I: completed shop (houses) with street frontages provide economic opportunities

* Llewelyn-Davies Kinhill Pty Ltd., with Sy Cip Corres Velayo & Co. The Second Feasibility Study of Dagat-Dagatan and Regional Centers, Final Report, July 1978.

Dagat-Dagatan, phase I: completed house (left) and unextended core (right)

relocation of a family is the completion of a functioning sanitary core on site.
4 Simpler, cheaper, on-plot provision was universally preferred because it gave families greater planning freedom at lower cost.

These conclusions were drawn following a series of residents' meetings at which a full range of options and approximate costs were presented to the residents in isometric sketch form. There was a very close, but independent, correlation of preferences amongst the resident groups.

Based on the clear direction given by the survey findings, and the imperative need to reduce costs, the modified distribution is being applied through subsequent phases, i.e. phase II A/B (balance of 3,500 plots), phase 3 (9,000 plots), and ultimately phase 4 (about 2,750 plots).

(IX) Dwelling Improvement and Extension

Approval of designs for permanent dwellings is granted by the Project Office planning staff after consideration of formal plans and details submitted with written documentation by the families themselves. Staff are available to advise and assist with such submissions and additional staff can be recruited to meet growing demands in the future.

Since on-plot provision for allottees generally represents only a small part of the completed dwelling, each family undertakes most of the building operation itself, in many cases with help from subcontractors and specialists within the community. The pace of construction varies widely in accordance with income, available savings and opportunity. Many relocated families have built temporary, shanty-type shelters, utilizing the sanitary core and lean-to roof provided, to enable them to occupy the plot pending availability of funds for permanent improvements. Elsewhere substantial two-storey houses are completed within 3 to 7 months of relocation. The temporary structures, although anticipated, cause the project management some concern because the use of light-weight scrap materials and low party-wall standards create the risk of fire and collapse. For this reason, NHA will establish the maximum length of time permitted for beneficiaries to retain their temporary structures, after which they will be required to construct a more permanent structure in accordance with established building regulations.

Chapter 2

Planning Sites and Services Projects

2.1 Target Groups

In designing sites and services projects it is extremely important to identify and recruit appropriate target groups. From the people's side it is important that the project really matches their priorities and preferences in the related areas of employment, savings and housing. From the project implementation side it is necessary to make sure that the people it ultimately recruits and relocates to the project site can meet their financial commitments, thus enabling the project to maximize cost recovery.

For the poorest of the low income groups, day to day survival is the main and primary concern. This means that employment opportunities are the paramount consideration. Housing quality is much less important. A housing arrangement that is proximate to the best income opportunities and flexible enough to enable a move to another, better employment opportunity is what these very poor seek. Also, it is usually true that such people have very little money to invest in housing. Renting a minimal shack in a slum is less of a burden than paying off a plot and core house in a sites and services project.

The project agencies need to bring into their schemes people who are poor and in need of housing but who are also able and willing to pay for what they are getting and to invest in the subsequent development of their housing. This strategy does, after all, place quite high demands on the families who are selected. They are called on to make serious long-term financial commitments (including a substantial downpayment) and, as well, they must direct money (and often their own labour) into the completion and extension of the house. When a sites and services project is being implemented along with slum upgrading schemes, there is good justification for believing that the latter is more appropriately directed to the very poor whilst the former is addressed to the slightly more advantaged among the low income groups. The selection of prospective clients for sites and services projects must take low income and housing needs into account, but it must also consider the potential of the applying family to survive in the new housing arrangement that is being offered to it.

Thorough surveys of household incomes and expenditures, present housing conditions and employment can be useful to clarify perceptions of which families might benefit from the project. However, many difficulties hamper the collection of reliable information about family incomes and expenditure patterns. Moreover, because sites and services schemes often recruit clients from a large city segment (or on a city-wide basis) rather than from a particular existing slum community, it is not easy to ascertain potential clients' real ability and willingness to pay on a community basis. Strategies to achieve the latter could include liaison between slum upgrading departments and sites and services project designers about a particular community and its general economic situation, or it could involve consultation with the credit union or other community organization that might be functioning in such a community. In any event, whatever the data limitations, it is important that project designers attempt to clarify income and expenditure patterns in order to design the financial arrangements for a sites and services project. One crucial point that has been too often overlooked or underestimated is the impact that the move to a new housing location has on a family's ability to pay.

Generally speaking, sites and services projects also aim to set up cohesive and viable communities that will be competent and responsible in managing their own affairs, including such things as maintenance, community facilities and activities, and organizing effectively to bargain for appropriate ongoing development of services. Also, in some countries where project target groups are comprised of mixed and potentially hostile religious and ethnic subgroups, relevant data should be obtained to ensure that fair, rational and appropriate selection takes place. If due regard is not paid to these matters, the implementation and long-term success of the project will be jeopardized.

Another issue in the selection of families for sites and services projects is whether there should be a uniform (or fairly narrow) range of income levels included or whether it is better to design for a wider range of low to middle income groups. It is difficult actually to restrict a project to a very narrow range of income levels. One advantage of designing the project for a range of low to middle income groups is that it enables the more innovative and realistic marketing of variously priced plots of different sizes and with different locational advantages within the project site. This, in turn, can facilitate the use of cross-subsidies within the project and thus render it accessible to even lower percentiles of low income families. In this sense the inclusion of some better-off low income families, or even middle income families, enables the project to avail poorer families of better housing opportunities. However, there is a trade-off involved. Every plot of land allotted to a higher income family means that one plot less is available to really low income families. Moreover, plots attractive to better-off families from middle income groups are likely to be larger, so the ratio between land offered to lower income groups and middle income groups may be even more unfavourable. However, from the design point of view the inclusion of better-off families certainly enhances cost recovery because of their greater ability to pay.

The latter point raises the issue of the economic viability of the community that is being created through a sites and services project. If only very low income families are selected, there is a strong possibility that a ghetto of the poor will result with consequent economic and social problems. A mix of income groups, on the other hand, generates income opportunities for lower income households. These opportunities, such as vending, washing, housekeeping, scavenging, and other forms of marginal employment, though lowly paid, provide an important income supplement for low income families. In a recent World Bank publication, the danger of uniformly low income sites and communities was noted:

> One real danger, for example, is that those eligible for plots may be limited by design and selection criteria to a fairly narrow band of the income distribution of a city. To some extent this danger can be averted through better design and by the encouragement, through various financial incentives, of some higher income groups to settle within these communities. Governments and other sponsoring institutions, however, are understandably reluctant to divert their efforts and resources to fulfilment of the needs of higher income groups. (Churchill, 1980, p.19)

The initial argument in this quotation is valid and useful in terms of project design, but if actual expenditure can be deemed to reflect spending priorities, it appears that government agencies are not always reluctant to divert their efforts and resources to higher income groups. On the contrary, at government level the satisfaction of middle and higher income needs is often a greater priority than satisfying the needs of the poor. This is borne out by the enormous government expenditures, for example on roads, which primarily benefit the more affluent car owning families in the Third World cities. Also at the agency/bureaucratic level the natural and traditional tendency is to look after clients from the same socio-economic levels as the bureaucrats themselves.

Notwithstanding these trade-offs, it appears that some degree of income level mixing is desirable. However, care should be taken to identify all the subsidies that may be involved in a project and to ensure that direct and indirect subsidies are not passed on to income groups that do not really need them. Too often, project designers have little awareness of the trade-offs involved and this, in turn, leads to serious difficulties in the implementation stage.

2.2 Scale and Location

One of the major reasons for government agencies abandoning conventional construction and undertaking slum upgrading and sites and services approaches is to achieve scale. This means that the numbers of families involved in specific projects and the overall numbers involved in slum improvement programmes and sites and services projects must bear some significance in relation to the target population as a whole. If average conditions are to be measurably improved, the slum improvement programme and sites and services projects as a whole should be large enough in scale to meet backlogs of improved housing needed as well as the demand resulting from national population growth, rural-urban migration and social changes such as reduction in household sizes. Indeed, if the scale is insufficient to meet these needs, then only a slowing in deterioration of housing conditions in existing squatter settlements will be achieved.

The issue of scale of sites and services projects immediately necessitates consideration of land availability within a given city. It is often the case that the areas of unoccupied land available in inner city areas are rather small and, because of their attractive location, very expensive. However, in some cities, for example Bangkok, there are large areas of rather centrally located land available that seem to be not particularly suitable for commercial development because of their location deep inside the narrow *sois* (side streets), away from the main thoroughfares where most commercial and business developments are located. In such cities a choice can be made as to where to locate sites and services projects. Whenever possible this choice should be made carefully and with due consideration for its impact on the intended residents' ability to survive economically in their new location and to improve their economic standing to the degree that they can develop their houses accordingly.

Too often in the past, sites and services projects have been located far from city centres. This has been justified on the grounds that peripheral land is cheaper and, in some cities, significant tracts of fringe land are in government ownership already. But there are several disadvantages to such locations that must be confronted. In several project experiences where peripheral locations have been used, the target population has not moved out onto the new site because of the limited access to employment opportunities in the city proper. Clearly, access to employment opportunities, either through proximity or cheap transportation, is a fundamental ingredient for a satisfactory housing arrangement for low income families.

Another disadvantage of peripheral and remote locations is that they lie beyond the reach of existing urban infrastructure networks and so the provision of basic utilities such as water supply, sewerage, and electricity is disproportionately, sometimes even prohibitively, expensive. This means either that cost recovery is retained and the cost burden is passed on to the project participants (with probable disruption of target group selection), or that cost recovery is to be at least partially sacrificed to achieve target group priorities in the short run. (In the long run, sacrificing replicability limits the numbers of low income families that can benefit.) One way to overcome this serious financial burden on peripherally located sites and services projects is to develop a policy whereby such off-site infrastructure as trunk mains for water supply and sewerage, circuit main lines for electricity supply and major road linkages to the city are not charged to the project but borne by the state or municipal authority as is indeed the case for most of the other developed areas of cities.

The alternative to large peripheral site locations is to utilize many smaller sites in intermediate locations. Whilst several sites could conceivably be more costly to prepare and administer, it is more likely that they could draw on relevant target groups from the immediate vicinities who could continue to make their livelihoods in a familiar neighbourhood. Furthermore, because they would probably have access to existing utility and service networks, they may provide a competitive unit price (despite higher land cost) as against large schemes in remote locations. And certainly the project would not be burdened with an income generation (employment provision) component that is costly to implement and uncertain in outcome. Another advantage of small to medium project sites in intermediate locations is that they are more manageable. The day to day management of site preparation, core house construction and community facilities is easier and the families themselves have more access to skilled labour and building materials for house development.

Very large projects and groups of smaller projects administered simultaneously by the same agency are difficult to manage. It is much harder to muster sufficient resources, ranging from experienced personnel to building materials, and to maintain momentum on a very large scale. The style of site management that is required for self help projects is different from that required for the conventional building industry. There is a social dimension to the task that is as important as the technical one, and government officials who are efficient and diligent site managers and who, as well, have goodwill and concern for their clients are hard to find. The supply of building materials to large remote sites is complicated by the often limited availability and the high demand from more affluent buyers for such materials. In many of the countries in which sites and services projects discussed in this book are operating, there are booming black markets for such products, and government quota systems, more often than not, exacerbate rather than eradicate such practices.

Small-scale projects (be they in intermediate or peripheral locations) are fairly limited in the range of plot size options they can offer. In contrast, large-scale projects with a variety of plot size options and efficient land utilization provide more opportunities for cross-subsidies. These can in turn help projects reach down to families from lower income percentiles without sacrificing cost recovery, provided that adequate employment access can be arranged. Nevertheless, it would be possible to achieve a similar range of plot size options within a group of smaller, more centrally located projects.

Another drawback to achieving scale in sites and services projects, when utilizing several smaller but more centrally located sites, is the matter of land acquisition. It is likely that more complicated and protracted acquisition arrangements will be encountered in such cases. Besides the costs that can be attributed to the delay itself, there are also expenses pertaining to compensation of landlords, lessees and even squatter communities that may be occupying parts of the selected site. With peripherally located land such problems are far less frequent, because the land is often under agricultural use and sparsely populated.

It is important that the choice of project location should be made realistically with the above trade-offs in mind. Too often, only peripheral locations have been considered, based exclusively on the perceived availability of fairly low-cost land which can be easily acquired. Such one-sided consideration often generates further defective decisions concerning project design, such as neglect of the provision of transportation services (which it may be necessary to subsidize in the initial years), employment generation and other vital supports to incoming residents. Land selection should be made with close reference to the ultimate project aims and with the future community's interests in mind, and shall not be based just on short-term considerations like raw cost per square metre and convenience of acquisition.

2.3 Scope and Standards

The sites and services strategy resulted from the perception that it is inequitable to extend high standards and a comprehensive range of benefits to a tiny fraction of the urban poor, when it is possible to design projects that utilize more economic minimum standards providing basic housing for a much larger number of those in need. The fundamental task is the preparation of newly urbanized land in economical plot sizes on which lower income families can develop their housing. Indeed, this has to be kept squarely in mind lest too many other components append themselves to sites and services projects and consequently drive up the unit cost to the implementing agency, and finally to the incoming residents.

In order to offset this natural but counterproductive tendency to increase project complexity, it is worthwhile to review what the essential components of sites and services projects are, and what components are more optional or specifically necessary, on a case by case basis. Apart from raw urban land, there is a definite need for certain infrastructural components. These include land levelling (where necessary), site planning, water and electricity supply, drainage and sewage disposal systems, garbage collection and an access system (both pedestrian and vehicular). In practice, these components constitute the major part of the total project cost.

However, there is also a wide range of social and economic services and facilities which may have to be provided within the scope of the project if they are not already available in the project's vicinity. These include health and education facilities, sites for markets, commercial activities and police stations, and even industrial developments that can provide employment for project families. Again, the degree to which they are vital to a project's viability will depend very much on whether they already exist outside the project itself but within reasonable distances from it. Not all of these items need necessarily be cost burdens to the project itself, and it is important to good project design to ensure that, whenever possible, they are designed to be self-sufficient or even profitable to the project.

Educational facilities are usually developed and administered by the local educational authorities, thus incurring no initial or long-term financial burden to the project itself. Industrial development on project lands can also be designed in such a way as to be saleable at a net profit to the project while, at the same time, offering an attractive investment to industrial entrepreneurs. However, the planning of industrial estates is quite complex and involves compromises of project goals with entrepreneurs' interests. (See case studies I and VIII for discussion and analysis of these compromises.) Beyond these project components there is the question of core houses. It is worth restating that the provision of core housing is not a necessary feature of sites and services projects as the strategy is not to deliver housing but rather the basis for the development of housing. In some of the most successful experiences in Africa, for example in Tanzania, there are no core houses provided. New projects there are planned to provide only a surveyed plot and water through public kiosks, each one catering for 350 plots (Rodell, 1981).

As a main element in the sites and services approach is to maximize the self help contribution in the development of housing, project residents should be given as much freedom as possible in choosing what to build. Ideally, this should be reflected in building regulations that restrain householders from dangerous or disruptive construction rather than prescribe exclusively what can be built.

> The emphasis here could be determining minimum limits within which the builders can exercise as large a degree of choice as is consistent with an economical use of the land and socially desirable neighbourhoods. Limits on spatial positioning, and on the use of certain materials, will however, be needed to cover general safety considerations. Where earthquake hazards are serious and where population densities are high, more severe limitations will be needed. But the traditional detailed building codes and materials specifications applicable to contractor-built conventional housing are likely to be quite inappropriate and involve far too heavy costs for the settler. (International Bank for Reconstruction and Development, 1974, p.11)

By and large, then, dwelling design and the selection of materials should be left in the hands of the dwellers themselves. If there is to be a core house, it should be of a design that can be easily extended later on. Rigid designs will make the project unit unattractive to users and this will lead to wastage at later stages when families have to knock down core house walls in order to develop housing space appropriate to their needs. Similarly, extensions made at a later point in time should be guided by general safety principles rather than strict prescriptive building regulations. The experience in this regard has been that if projects lay down strict prescriptive rules, involving what residents perceive to be unwarranted curtailment of their extension options and unnecessary expense, then occupants will breach those rules. (See case study VI for an example of this phenomenon.)

It is important that government agencies adopting the sites and services strategy perceive that standards for public housing construction projects are inappropriate to the new task. Modified and upgradable standards appropriate to sites and services projects should reflect the modified role of the planning agency.

> Firstly, the sites and services strategy does not have the same technology indivisibilities as conventional housing. With the latter, everything has to come together in the final form at once. House, sewerage, water, electricity, roads, open spaces are each built today and built to last for a long time. Each requires full financing today. In contrast, sites and services can be developed incrementally, and each major infrastructural element can be developed incrementally. Simple projects need have nothing but water. Government can install water for a variety of service standards and, if it starts with low standards, it can raise standards over time. Low initial standards and costs do not build in permanently low quality as they do with conventional housing. (Rodell, 1981, p.7)

Initial designs and standards for most infrastructural items should be set in such a way as to allow gradual or later development. Roads and pathways can initially be built with a temporary surface, both in terms of depth (thickness) and width, which will suffice for a certain length of time. Items like street lighting may also be of lower standard initially. However, in the case of underground utilities usually a permanent design should be followed (particularly if subsequent upgrading would require the digging up of sealed roads and walkways).

The Asian project experience suggests the following guidelines for arriving at standards for infrastructural components:

1 Roads and pathways: the right of way should be minimal depending on local government regulations but with potential for later upgrading. The initial specifications should not be of a permanent nature.
2 Water supply: 100 to 130 litres per person per day with 12 to 16 hours' supply. (Of course, this may not be feasible in some countries.) Individual connections are recommended because there is usually wastage from community stand-pipes.
3 Sewerage: underground sewerage systems are recommended for large projects provided they are not prohibitively expensive. In smaller projects septic tanks may be suitable. Pit latrines are recommended in locations where soil conditions permit effective soakage.
4 Drainage: open drains with lining to minimize clearing and maintenance problems are adequate.
5 Electricity: individual connections only if the majority of residents so

desire. For road and path lighting systems the prevailing rules should be adhered to. (However, electricity supply at usual standards is normally feasible in most places.)

6 Social facilities need not be completed before the families start moving onto project sites. Community facilities can be developed gradually depending on the demands created by the people living on the new site. An intrinsic advantage to this approach is that it will enable the community itself to participate in the design and possibly the financing and construction of these facilities. This implies, though, that the settlers in the early phases may have to experience some degree of privation until sufficient demand justifies the installation and expansion of these facilities.

7 On the matter of land use it is important that this expensive and non-renewable resource be utilized economically. The larger the plots and the larger the areas set aside for community facilities, the higher the cost of land per plot. As a rule of thumb, at least 70 per cent of project land should be saleable for residential, commercial or industrial use, with the remaining 30 per cent or less to be used for circulation, community facilities, and open spaces.

2.4 Planning for Cost Recovery and Replicabilty

Cost recovery is an important goal of sites and services projects because it is perceived that good housing solutions must be replicable on a large scale. Complete cost recovery is not always feasible and the evidence to date suggests that the task is more one of reducing subsidies to sustainable levels in the long term, spread across a large number of low income people. But certainly subsidies should be recognized, trimmed down, and directed only to those who cannot manage without them.

First and foremost, this necessitates the consideration of the real costs of the project on the one hand and the income levels and ability and willingness to pay of the target group on the other. All elements of real costs must be identified even when they are hidden and difficult to calculate. This is necessary so that whatever subsidies may be involved can be calculated and distributed appropriately to the largest number of disadvantaged families.

Calculating the ability of target groups to pay for whatever housing arrangement the project provides is, in itself, quite complex and prone to error. Using income data to determine ability to pay is not reliable, due to the possible understatement of income by low income groups and overstatement of the poverty of people who, on account of yearly variations in their income, may have been classified as poor when on the average they are not. Ability to pay may be related not only to minimum income levels, but also to minimum levels of expenditures. The use of expenditure levels is more relevant in that such levels take into consideration the operative income transfer mechanisms of society: the family, religious and other charitable institutions, and government welfare services. Ability to pay for housing requires savings for downpayments as well as sufficient resources to make regular monthly payments. When the level of savings is low, it is difficult for families to meet the down payments, which are usually substantial. The financing of such mortgage and loans is often highly institutionalized and conventional so that little adjustment is made to suit the special needs of the poor. In the Vashi project in Bombay, the Housing and Urban Development Corporation (HUDCO) insists on not funding more than two thirds of the costs, which leads to the unreasonably high down payments of one third of the unit cost (see case study V). In cases where levels of savings are low, special measures have to be formulated for either staggering the down payment into two or three instalments, reducing it or dispensing with it altogether. Appropriate adjustments must automatically be made to maintain the project's cash flow.

It must be remembered also that moving to a new location will bring changes, initially more often problematical than ameliorative, to household incomes and expenditures. For example, moving to peripheral locations will usually bring increased expenditure on transportation to places of work related to the household's old location, and higher costs for day to day supplies of food and other household commodities. Moreover, time that families might put into developing their core houses might well cut down on their income earning opportunities in the form of overtime in their normal jobs or reduced hours available for vending and other kinds of informal employment.

In calculating monthly repayment arrangements, therefore, a cautious approach is needed, because large-scale defaults on repayments ultimately have the same destructive impact on cost recovery that excessive subsidies have. Conventional estimates, which set households' monthly ability to pay for housing at 20–25 per cent of their income, are more reliable in some contexts than others. It is important to remember that the poorer the people, the lower the percentage of their monthly incomes they can afford to spend on housing. This particularly applies to low income people in sites and services projects: besides their having to make a monthly payment for their plot and the infrastructure that services it, money is needed for skilled labour and materials to develop their housing and for maintenance. Sometimes not all these factors are considered. Indeed, project designers should take special care that the financial design of the project does not actually impoverish the families it sets out to assist through shackling them to housing payments that they cannot afford. This possibility can be kept at bay through careful analysis in the planning phase of the issues raised above, as well as through realistic design of the formal and informal employment generating components of the project.

Besides realistically calculating the target group's ability to pay, it is also necessary to cost accurately all the components of a project if cost recovery and replicability are to be achieved. In many projects this has not been done. Elements of real project costs often not reflected in sites and services costing policies include market land price, off-site infrastructure (in so far as it directly benefits the scheme), administrative overheads, interest on beneficiaries' loans, and cost contingency.

Unless real costs are identified and calculated, a rational pricing policy which seeks to retain a maximum feasible level of cost recovery cannot be formulated. Such a policy, based upon real costs and the clients' ability to pay, will reflect differential land values related to different locations and differences in standards of development in the sites and services scheme, thus enabling subsidies to go to the most appropriate group. Such cross subsidies do not harm cost recovery. Market rates charged for better located plots, plots with superior infrastructure or superstructure, as well as for commercial and industrial land use will create a surplus which may be utilized for below cost provision of the poorest options. This should be fully utilized because it enables the economically disadvantaged to gain access to housing.

Over and above the issues raised so far there are several other planning issues that can incur unnecessary expenses for the project, disrupt cash flow, and ultimately reduce the chances of maximizing cost recovery. These are inadequate interagency coordination mechanisms, inefficient allocation criteria leading to untimely allocation of plots, and lack of planning for appropriate payment collection procedures and for hedging against inflation.

The matter of coordinating activities by the agencies involved is of primary concern to project planning (this is discussed in detail in Chapter 3). Unless clear and reliable interagency procedures are set up before project implementation is underway, the efficient scheduling of ongoing activities and decision making is impossible. One way to achieve this is to involve all concerned agencies as early as possible in the project planning stage.

Allocation criteria and procedures should be carefully designed so as to enable the occupation of plots as soon as they become available. Allocation of all plots need not be carried out at once. It can be done on a phase by phase basis as different phases of the project become available for occupation. Another approach is to allot plots well before the site has been prepared to give the families time to save up for their down payment, and to prepare themselves in terms of finding new jobs in the project's vicinity before the probably traumatic shift to their new housing situation. However, this is often difficult in view of the limited credibility of housing agencies in many developing countries in the eyes of the public. The result in such cases may well be a total disbelief that the project will ever be implemented. In order to offset such a response, a thorough public relations campaign would be necessary.

The planning of collection procedures also requires due care. They should not place excessive burdens in terms of loss of time and costs for transportation on the paying households. Neither should they involve unnecessary administrative inputs on the part of the project's collection agency. Rather, they should be streamlined to facilitate payment, collection, and follow-up in cases of default. Furthermore, it is vital to retain the residents' goodwill by making the financial arrangements of the project clear to them; it is especially important that they know what they are paying for.

Beyond budgeting for price contingencies, inflationary factors are generally beyond the control of good project design, but inflation should be kept in mind as it can contribute to cash flow problems. In a country where the inflation rate is high, fixed monthly payments may form a decreasing proportion of monthly household expenditures over time. However, if food prices and transportation costs are rising faster than incomes, families may still face increased difficulties in meeting their repayment commitments, with negative consequences for the project's cash flow. Inflation must also be taken into account when calculating project maintenance changes for project residents. Failure to take this into consideration can affect the replicability of the project.

2.5 Community Participation, Employment Generation, and Self Help

Sites and services projects, in addition to providing land and basic services, are intended to foster community participation in their design and implementation, so as to ensure cooperation between the residents and the concerned agencies and ultimately to develop the community economically and socially. Community participation is important to the appropriate design of a project in terms of the location of the project, its designed habitat opportunities and standards, its in-project employment generation programme, and the social services and facilities it provides. Of course, it is vital to the smooth implementation of the project, especially in the areas of plot or core house development, maintenance, and the repayment programmes. There are, however, real difficulties in designing projects and implementing them in such a way as to stimulate and utilize people's participation, especially when the future project residents are not being recruited directly from a particular slum or low income community.

It is not something that follows automatically even if procedural adjustments have been made to enable the people to participate. It involves environmental and attitudinal changes in the agency or agencies involved in the project. On the environmental side it means recruiting and developing skilled staff who are able to go out into the slum communities from whence the target group is to be drawn, mix sympathetically with the people, win their confidence, and encourage and reassure them in the ongoing process of dialogue with project designers and administrators. Besides requiring these specially trained community-oriented staff to enlist community participation, agencies need much better coordination (less bureaucratic and control-oriented and more flexible and dynamic) between the planners, architects, economists, community organizers, and social workers involved.

It is worth noting that the employment components in sites and services projects have usually been only partially successful in meeting the employment needs of the families allotted plots in those projects. This has been partly a result of inadequate institutional mechanisms for attracting entrepreneurs to the project area, and partly a result of insufficient understanding of the precise employment needs of the project population. Clearly, closer involvement of the target community in project design could help overcome the latter by enabling better identification of the people (and their skills) and the subsequent setting up of suitable employment opportunities for them. In so far as offering economically attractive opportunities to industrial entrepreneurs is required, it is important to ensure that such incentives be linked to guarantees from the companies concerned to draw a significant number of its employees, 70 per cent for example, from the project community. Furthermore, exemption from legal minimum wage payment should not be included in the package of incentives offered, because this would be against the interests of the project households and the project goals themselves. The paramount design idea in handling the employment component is to assist the project families to improve themselves economically so they can pay for their units, develop savings, and gradually develop the size and quality of their shelter.

This self help phase or family managed development of the plot or core house, besides concerning the families themselves, bears directly on the roles of the estate management staff (including technical advisers and building inspectors). Therefore, it is most appropriate that they, together with the target group households, should contribute to the design process. In this way, wasteful and impractical designs and their consequent, unenforceable building regulations will not be inflicted on the families and the estate management authorities respectively. Appropriate core housing design and minimal building rules can maximize the family's mobilization of resources to develop its house efficiently and, at the same time, minimize the chances of conflict and the need for supervision of the self help phase.

2.6 Case Study Focus

The first case study in this chapter is the sites and services component of the Bang Plee Bang Bor new town. This project, which is in its initial stages of implementation, is the fourth and largest venture by the National Housing Authority of Thailand into sites and services. From a planning point of view it is of considerable interest because it draws on the experiences of two earlier sites and services projects, Rangsit and Tung Song Hong.* These latter projects suffered from serious design weaknesses, most importantly in their financial structure and in their types of core housing. The Bang Plee Bang Bor project, however, has been much more carefully thought out, but it is also a much more ambitious project in so far as it undertakes to provide large-scale employment opportunities on site.

The second case study is the Gujaini site and services project in Kanpur. The project, which is part of phase I of the Kanpur Urban Development Project,

---

* The design process for the third sites and services project of the National Housing Authority of Thailand, Lad Krabang, was carried out almost simultaneously with that of Bang Plee Bang Bor and so, in terms of experience, contributed very little to the design of the latter.

was about to select participants at the time of the seminar, but allocations were not to be made until infrastructure was completed some 9 months later. The waiting period was planned to enable intending residents to consolidate their downpayments and prepare themselves for the move to the project site. This project also demonstrates various planning strategies within the sites and services approach to reach the very poor without indulging in heavy subsidies.

Case Study II BANG PLEE BANG BOR, BANGKOK

(I) Background

In 1979 the Bangkok metropolis had an estimated population of 4.9 million with an annual growth rate of 3.3 per cent. The city is the national capital, and contains the country's major port, most of the secondary and tertiary educational institutions, modern hospitals and clinics. It is also the centre of commerce and industry and, because of the wide range of employment opportunities it provides, the city has experienced rapid population growth, particularly in the last three decades. Utilities, services, and facilities have not been able to keep pace with demand and an estimated 30 per cent of the population live in crowded and unserviced areas.

Despite the rapid growth rate of Bangkok, there has been no serious intervention in terms of town planning and therefore urban sprawl continues unabated. Typical land use follows the extensions of utility development in a haphazard pattern with mixed use of land. The main problem of Bangkok is the serious inadequacy of urban facilities such as roads, drainage systems, water supply, and also social services such as health care, educational services and housing.

The metropolis is expanding mostly in northerly and easterly directions, where major roads provide the main linkages. However, the existing built-up area of the metropolis is the main source of employment and it remains heavily populated. The traffic problem, overcrowded communities and a polluted environment are reasons why some areas of Bangkok are considered to be unsuitable places for living.

In 1940 the government began to react to the housing problem but its efforts were sporadic and lacking in firm policy, forward planning and resource allocation rationale. The demand for housing was very high, especially for low income people who migrated from rural areas. The estimated 1977–1982 housing demand is 241,000 units. The private sector can supply only 166,000 units and will leave 75,000 units for the public sector to handle.

In 1973 the National Housing Authority (NHA) was established by unifying four housing agencies. At the time they were able to produce only some 8,700 welfare housing units. Most of them were rental walk-up apartments, which involved fairly substantial subsidies to meet the low income families' affordability. The NHA continued producing this type of house until 1975. At that time, an attempt was made to develop more effective policy guidelines, supporting the government policy that housing should be among the nation's top priorities.

In 1976 the NHA 5-year plan (1976–1980) to produce 120,000 units was approved. From the fiscal year 1978, the NHA proposed a revised housing programme with substantially reduced subsidy requirements and lowered development targets. It also included sites and services and slum upgrading in the programme.

Bang Plee new town project represents a radical departure from most of the earlier subsidized projects because it is almost free of direct subsidy. Instead, a cross-subsidy is planned. Government subsidies will be given in the form of off-site and (some) on-site infrastructure and community facilities only.

(II) Agencies Involved in Design and Implementation

The principal institutions responsible for urban planning and development are the Bangkok Metropolitan Authority (BMA), the Town and Country Planning Office (TCPO), and the Industrial Estate Authority of Thailand (IEAT); and for housing, the NHA and the Government Housing Bank (GHB). Infrastructural services are provided by the Metropolitan Electricity Authority (MEA) and the Metropolitan Water Works Authority (MWWA). The National Economic and Social Development Board (NESDB) bears overall responsibility for economic and social planning and for the allocation of funds under Thailand's National Economic and Social Development Plan.

The executing agency for the project's housing and for all of the project infrastructure facilities is the NHA, who will act in collaboration with other government agencies and supervise the construction of the project's housing and all civil engineering infrastructure, including land development, road works, stormwater drainage, water supply, sewerage, and community facilities such as parks and schools. NHA will act in consultation with MWWA with respect to water supply and with IEAT concerning the industrial estate proposed in the project. Supervision of the design and construction of the electricity distribution system will be carried out for the NHA by the MEA. Telephone services are to be provided under the project by the Telephone Organization of Thailand and will be financed and managed by it.

Upon completion of the project, NHA will be responsible for the general urban management of the project's housing and commercial areas until such time as a municipal authority is directed, or created, to take over this function. However, responsibility for the operation and maintenance of the project's water and power services will rest with MWWA and MEA respectively. IEAT will be responsible for operating and maintaining the industrial estate and will levy a charge to cover the costs involved from the factories in the estate. The project's schools, upon their completion, will be operated and maintained by the Ministry of Education.

(III) Project Aims and Target Groups

The project is part of the government's programme to relieve the nation's urban housing deficiencies. The programme's general aims are to reduce regional inequalities in employment opportunities, to offset the urban dominance of Bangkok and to relieve its extreme shortage of housing, especially for lower income groups, through the provision of improved housing and employment opportunities in other urban centres. This entails the creation of planned settlements and new towns where appropriate, in cooperation with the IEAT, on the outer fringe of Bangkok. Bang Plee Bang Bor is one such new town.

After all three phases are complete, the resident population is expected to comprise 21,500 families or 120,000 persons. The expected income distribution is shown in Table 1.

Table 1 Expected income distribution of families in Bang Plee Bang Bor

% of families	Monthly income levels (US$) at 1979 prices
23.72	below 125
30.88	125–<175
21.82	175–<225
15.81	225–<325
7.77	above 325

The development of the new town includes the creation of an industrial estate and commercial centre together with necessary community facilities and services, as well as government and local administrative agencies. These together are expected to provide job opportunities on site for 19,000 people (see Table 2). Some 21,000 jobs off-site are also expected within a reasonable commuting distance of 20 kilometres.

Table 2 Expected job opportunities in Bang Plee Bang Bor

Opportunities in:	Jobs
Industrial plants	7,200
Hospital, health service, and clinic	150
Commercial centre	7,970
Education services	1,300
Domestic services (hired by higher income residents)	2,000
Government employment	380
Total	19,000

(IV) Site Selection, Land Acquisition, and Scheduled Development (Phase I)

The land selected for the new town lies between Bangkok and Samut Prakarn, a small town about 30 kilometres south-east of Bangkok. In the last decade this district has been experiencing a change of land use from agricultural to scattered industrial and commercial use along main roads like Sukhumvit Road and the Bangna-Trad expressway.

The 716.32 hectares site was selected from a number of similar properties in its vicinity for US$0.55 per square metre in 1976. The site depends mainly on Teparak Road, the Bangna-Trad expressway, and the *klongs* (canals) traversing the site for passenger and cargo transportation to Bangkok. Klong Samrong, navigable throughout the year, links the site to the Chao Phya River. The nearest established local authority within the province is the Samut Prakarn municipality. There is no piped water supply or sewerage facility.

The site, like most properties in and near metropolitan Bangkok, is low lying and flood prone and requires considerable development in terms of drainage. After exploring several options, the NHA decided on building a dyke 1.5 metres high and digging a ditch 1.5 metres deep around most of the site, installing a pumping station, and using land fill for the area north of Teparak Road. The cost of the land after development amounted to about US$10.00 square metre.

The project is to be developed in three phases during 1980-1990. The first phase (5,000 units on 266.3 hectares, 1980-1984) is currently being undertaken according to the following development stages.

The first stage (November 1980-November 1981) involves the construction of the flood protection system, land filling for some of the upper part of the project area, construction of the main road and the bridge crossing Klong Samrong.

The second stage (November 1981-December 1982) involves the development of 45 hectares of land, the construction of 3,162 units of core houses, 273 shophouses, community facilities (including four kindergartens/day-care centres, and NHA office, community playground and park), and the provision of on-site infrastructure.

The third stage (December 1982-December 1983) will entail the development of 18 hectares of land, the construction of 832 units of core houses, 20 shop-houses, more community facilities (including a school, a health centre, post offices and a library), and the provision of related on-site infrastructure.

The fourth stage (January 1984-December 1984) involves the development of 130 hectares of land and the construction of 878 core house units, 20 shophouses, and the outlying business centre. Further facilities and on-site infrastructure will also be completed.

During the implementation of these stages (between November 1980 and December 1983), 72.8 hectares of land will be developed by IEAT for an industrial estate with related infrastructure. The strategy is to develop the industrial estate gradually to meet the phase-wise growth of the community employment needs.

Data in the following sections relate to phase I of the new town project unless otherwise indicated.

(V) Planned Infrastructural Development

Roads and walkways in the new town are being designed to the width standards shown in Table 3 (see also site plan).

Table 3 Standards for roads and walkways in Bang Plee Bang Bor

Type		Width (m)	Vehicular lanes (m)	Walkways (m)	Median strip (m)	Remarks
Major road		32.0	16.00	5.50/5.50	5	Main spine road
Secondary road	A	18.0	12.00	3.00/3.00		Feeds off main road
	B	14.0	8.00	3.00/3.00		Feeds off secondary road A.
	C	14.0	9.00	2.50/2.50		Feeds off secondary road A.
Tertiary Road		7.5	4.50	1.50/1.50		Serves house frontages
Main pedestrian way		6.0	3.30	1.35/1.35		Serves house frontages
Secondary pedestrian way		4.0	2.00	1.00/1.00		Serves house frontages

The MWWA is authorized to provide water services to three provinces: the Bangkok Metropolitan Area, Nonthaburi, and Samut Prakarn. At present the MWWA's distribution network only services the built-up core area of the metropolis covering approximately 500 square kilometres. Outside the serviced area, deep wells are normally used in housing estates, whereas scattered agricultural households depend on rainwater, *klong* water, or pond water. Those households settled near the new town site are in the latter category. The MWWA's development plan up to the year 2000 envisages a system whereby 815 square kilometres of the metropolis will be served by a 'central system' of distribution with treated water from the Chao Phaya River. Outlying settlements will be served by eight separate systems. Bang Plee district centre will have one such systems and there will be another at Bang Bor district centre. These will be relatively modest systems drawing groundwater and serving populations of less than 10,000.

In May 1977 the Japan International Co-operation Agency (JICA) completed the 'Feasibility Study for the Separate System of Metropolitan

Water Supply in Bangkok', the proposals of which will most likely be accepted and adopted in the plans of the MWWA. This study took into account the existence of a new town at the proposed site on information supplied by the NHA. The JICA study concluded that a future water supply for the new town should be provided through an extension of the central system at Samrong that would transmit water to the new town through a 600 millimetre diameter pipe. It is planned that the central system water supply could be delivered from 1985; meanwhile, the new town would need to develop its own interim water supply through deep wells.

The discharge of untreated sewage from the new town could significantly affect the water quality of canals surrounding the project site. At present these waterways appear to provide a considerable harvest of fish. The water is also used for the irrigation of the adjacent rice fields. The project design includes a treatment facility which will produce an effluent having a BOD count of 20 ppm. While this is an excellent system, its operational costs are expected to be excessive due to anticipated increases in electricity rates. NHA engineers have designed a number of other systems for treating domestic sewage and will develop a suitable alternative to the system currently proposed. Consideration will be given to life cycle costing of alternative systems and to trade-offs between operational costs, capital costs, quality of effluent, and possible applications for aquaculture, as well as the additional land requirements of the various schemes evaluated. Among the systems commonly used in Bangkok is the individual septic tank. The design consists of a series of shallow tanks with an overflow into the stormwater drainage system.

Approximately 80 cubic metres of solid waste will be generated on the site per day and containerized storage will be sought from the outset. About 25 collection points will be established along the roads and main pedestrian walkways, each serving approximately 200 families. The containers located at each collection point are designed for a toal storage of 8 cubic metres, representing more than two days' collection. As in the case of other NHA development areas, Samut Prakarn municipality will be responsible for the regular removal of the waste from these containers.

The executing agency for electricity supply will be the MEA under instruction from NHA. MEA is responsible for the design and supervision of the construction of the electricity supply facility, but the design will be subject to NHA approval and NHA will liaise fully with MEA on all aspects.

At present, the MEA is installing a substation at Bang Plee district centre. It also plans to install one at Bang Bor district centre. Nevertheless, since the new town will be a large consumer of electrical power, these substations will not suffice. In particular, NHA will liaise with MEA with respect to additions to the existing transmission facilities to ensure that sufficient electricity will be available on site in time to meet the industrial consumer requirements for phase I of the project, and subsequently for phase II and phase III. The electricity facilities will be operated and maintained by MEA. Service connections will be installed by MEA after the installation fee has been

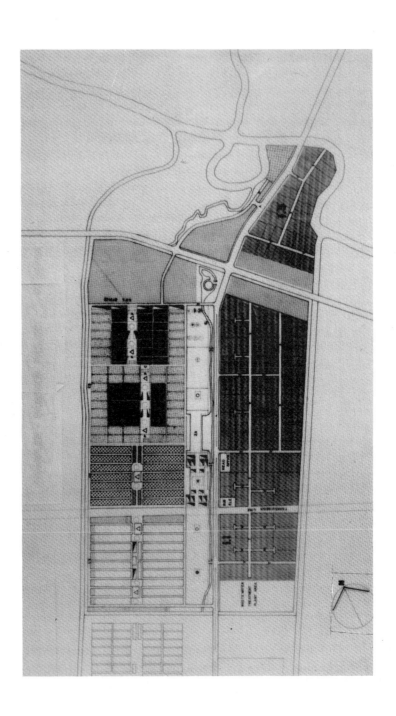

LAND USE PLAN

INCOME 1,500 - 2,000 BAHT / MONTH
INCOME 2,001 - 3,000 BAHT / MONTH
INCOME 3,001 - 4,000 BAHT / MONTH
INCOME 4,001 - 5,000 BAHT / MONTH
INCOME MORE THAN 6,000 BATH / MONTH
SHOPHOUSE
OUTLYING BUSINESS CENTRE
CENTRAL BUSINESS DISTRICT
BUS TERMINAL, BOAT LANDING
INDUSTRIAL ZONE
CORNER PARK
EDUCATIONAL AREA
TECNICAL COLLEGE
SECONDARY SCHOOL
PRIMARY SCHOOL
KINDERGARTEN
HOSPITAL
PLAZA
PARKING AREA
MAJOR PARK & OPEN SPACE

FOOD MARKET
BASKETBALL, BADMINTON, TENNIS COURT
ATHLETICS FIELD
POST OFFICE
TELEPHONE
DEEP WELL & WATER TOWER
YOUTH CENTRE
HEALTH CENTRE
FIRE STATION
FIRE HOSE & FIRE EXTINGUISHER
AREA OFFICE
PUBLIC HALL
POLICE STATION
POLICE BOOTH
MAIL BOX
COMMUNAL PLAYGROUND
HIGH VOLTAGE POST
THEATRE
TREATMENT PLANT
DIKE & DITCH

CANAL
LAKE
NEIGHBOURHOOD ROAD
DISTRIBUTOR ROAD
MAJOR ROAD
ARTERIAL ROAD
EXISTING ROAD
MAIN PEDESTRIAN & CYCLE TRACK
PEDESTRIAN & BICYCLE BRIDGE
BRIDGE
MAIN ROAD
SECONDARY ROAD
TERTIARY ROAD
MAJOR ROAD
TRANSMISSION LINE
TRAINING CENTRE

Bang Plee Bang Bor project, Bangkok

recovered from the applicant by MEA. Electricity charges will be recovered from the customer by MEA through normal billing procedures.

The project will provide one primary school, one secondary school and seven kindergarten/day-care centres at Bang Plee new town. The primary school and secondary school will absorb the projected 3,000 students in the vicinity and will work on a double-shift basis. Playgrounds and a football field will also be provided for the schools. A secondary health centre will be constructed on the site to supplement the existing centre and hospital in the area. The new centre will provide services including primary health care, an immunization programme, health education, maternal and child health care and family planning services. A community administration and services complex to be provided on the site will house an assembly hall, public library, youth centre, training centre, post office, the health centre, and office space. In addition, communal playgrounds and a park will be provided.

Public transportation will be provided by the Bangkok Mass Transit Authority. Bangna-Trad expressway and Teparak Road will have bus and minibus services to various industrial and commercial areas in the vicinity. The travelling time to most such places of employment is estimated at 20–40 minutes which is reasonable in terms of Bangkok traffic.

(VI) Land Use and Dwelling Options

As the project involves the creation of a new town together with an industrial estate and a commercial centre, the amount of land allocated to housing is somewhat lower than would be the case if it was situated within range of off-site employment generating centres and facilities. Some 4,691 core units, 109 house plots, and 309 shophouses will occupy 63.64 hectares or 23.6 per cent of the total site.

The industrial estate will occupy 73.67 hectares, 27.32 per cent of the total site, while the commercial centre will utilize 33.54 hectares or 12.44 per cent (see Table 6, p.67). Roads and walkways account for 32.25 hectares (11.96 per cent) and community facilities for 22.46 hectares (8.33 per cent). The remaining 44.09 hectares will be utilized for other infrastructural needs including the dyke system and utility station.

The project provides seven plot/dwelling options. Types A–D are core houses, type E is a large open plot, and the remaining two options are shophouses of two and three storeys. Types A and B are on identical plots of 84 m². Type A (1,260 units) has a core area of 25 m² which can be used by an incoming family as a multipurpose room, large enough to accommodate a six-person family at night and to serve as a kitchen/dining room/living area during the day. Only minor additions such as fitting doors and window shutters would be necessary before moving in. The plot, which is 4.2 m wide and 20 m in length will provide a variety of possible extensions. Type B (1,494 units) has a larger built core area of 38 m². Type C (1,060 units) is a two-storey core house of 48 m² in floor area on a plot of 160 m². Type D (768 units) is another two-storey core house of 48 m² in floor area on a 200 m² plot. Both these options, being on wider plots than types A and B, can be extended breadthwise and lengthwise. All core house units include a sanitary core. The last two options are two-storey (109 units) and three-storey (200 units) shophouses of 148 m² and 200 m² in floor area respectively. Both options are on small, narrow plots identical to types A and B. The type E open plot (109 plots) option is 440 m² in area.

The standards used have been restrained to the minimal requirements for a low income mass housing scheme, but only durable construction materials have been utilized in the core house design. Although the project is located outside the Bangkok metropolitan regulation control area, the design of residential and commercial buildings is generally based on the building regulations, but there are some items provided at lower standard, such as the thickness of the fire protection partition and the width of the staircase. A conventional construction system will be used for all core and shophouse options consisting of reinforced concrete beam and column structures with concrete block walls.

(VII) Allocation and Conditions of Purchase

The rent and hire purchase division of NHA's Estate Management Department will be responsible for sales of plots and units. Publicity campaigns will be undertaken for each phase. To be eligible for NHA housing, applicants must be Thai citizens resident in the city where the project is located, they must not own land or a house in the city, and they must meet the particular scheme's income criteria. It has been NHA's normal practice in earlier housing schemes to consider only the household head's income, although the spouse's income has also been counted if derived from regular wage employment. Income from informal or irregular employment or self-employment and the incomes of other household members have been ignored. This practice has led to considerable underestimation of household income for families with multiple earners. The NHA confirmed in its initial planning that it would assess the wage income of all regularly employed household members when screening applicants for units in this project.

Plots will be allocated approximately one year before they are ready for occupation to provide time for allottees to make down payments. In order to discourage speculative sales of plots, purchasers will be required to occupy their plots within 1 year of the time they are ready, and during the first 5 years resale will be restricted to NHA. However, purchasers will be allowed to let part of their unit to augment their incomes.

Type A is directed at a target group of income range below 2,000 baht* per month, at a projected sale price of 37,044 baht; type B at a target income group of 2,001–3,000 baht at a price of 50,923 baht; type C at a target

---

* US$1.00 = 23.05 baht (November 1981).

income group of 3,001–4,000 baht at a price of 79,576 baht. These three core house types will be purchased with a 10 per cent downpayment and monthly repayments over 20 years.

Type D is designed for a target income group of 4,000–6,000 baht at a price of 134,539 baht, and type E for a target income group of 6,000 baht at a price of 116,033 baht. Both will be purchased with a 20 per cent downpayment, but type D will be repaid at 14 per cent interest over 20 years whereas type E will be at 15 per cent over 15 years. The two-storey shophouses will sell for 278,580 and the three-storey shophouses for 366,238 baht. Both will require downpayments of 25 per cent with the balance repayable over 15 years at 15 per cent interest.

The proposal for the improvement and extension of dwelling units is to grant a cash loan for the residents to improve their own core units in the initial stage. The improvement or extension will be done on an individual basis. NHA will give technical assistance and control the standards of permanent structures.

Further proposals for the improvement and extension of core units will be initiated by the Estate Management Department. The roles of residents working together in extending their core units on a group basis have been seriously discussed. The community may be involved more in other activities. This will depend on proposals and future actions of the Estate Management Department and related agencies.

(VIII) Sources of funds

The sources of funds the project are shown in Table 4. The total project investment cost is US$61,893,250 which is the total cost of land acquisition and the development of infrastructure and community facilities, investment in industrial and commercial sites, core housing and overheads.

Table 4 Sources of funds for Bang Plee Bang Bor project

Loans from	Asian Development Bank	US$20,000,000 at 7% p.a.
	US AID	US$ 3,533,000 at 11% p.a.
	other agencies	US$16,273,450 at 14% p.a.
Grants from	Government of Thailand	US$10,199,750
	Telephone Organization of Thailand	US$ 2,766,200
Income during construction		US$ 9,120,850

Case Study III GUJAINI SITES AND SERVICES, KANPUR

(I) Background

Kanpur is the eighth largest city in India. It owes this position to the rapid industrialization which it underwent during the years 1919–1950. The textile and leather industries have played key roles in the Kanpur economy. The engineering industry is second in terms of output and employment after textiles, followed by the chemical and leather industries. According to the 1971 census, the Kanpur population was 1,275,000 (1980:1,595,000), and the labour force was of the order of 380,000 of which 34 per cent were employed in industry and more than 50 per cent in trade, commerce, and services sectors. The 37 large-scale industries and 536 small-scale units provide employment for 54,733 people in the organization sector, whereas employment in unregistered manufacturing units is approximately 40,000.

According to the 1971 census, the total number of residential houses in the Kanpur urban area was 243,400 and households numbered 268,500. Based on the current (1980) population estimates and an average family size of 4.94, there are 329,000 households in Kanpur. New household formation in Kanpur is currently estimated at about 10,000 per annum.

It is estimated that 500,000 persons (31 per cent of current population) may be living in slum-like conditions in Kanpur due to the inadequate response to their needs by the public sector. The development of urban land, whether public or private, is governed by master plan regulations and byelaws under Uttar Pradesh Urban Planning Development Act, 1973. At present the Kanpur Development Authority (KDA) is the only public agency which provides new housing stock. The KDA constructed 3,185 dwelling units up to March 1979 since its inception in 1974. In the year 1979–1980, KDA completed 3,252 dwelling units of various categories and, out of 7,152 units currently under construction, 4,311 were to be completed by March 1981. It is estimated that another 2,000 units are added per annum by the private sector.

For a number of years the government has given attention to the provision of housing for the low income population. It has also provided for the environmental improvement of slums.

(II) Aims of the Project

The aim of phase I of the Kanpur Urban Development Project is to promote programmes related to basic urban shelter specially for the economically weaker section (EWS) of the community. In this project, emphasis is being given to low-cost programmes that would be affordable to the EWS and low income group (LIG),* but nevertheless permitting cost recovery from the beneficiaries.

The main components of the Kanpur Urban Development Project (KUDP) are: (1) sites and services including employment promotion; (2) slum upgrading including technical services and training. Under the slum upgrading component, acquisition of *ahatas* (privately owned compounds), extension of on-site and off-site infrastructure, and granting of tenure to beneficiaries are

---

* Economically Weaker Section (EWS) is a term commonly used among Indian planners to describe the lowest-income groups. The term Low Income Group (LIG) is reserved for slightly better-off families. See also case studies IV, V, and VII.

the key objectives of the project, which seeks to achieve full cost recovery. Some 20,000 households will benefit from the slum upgrading programme.

The sites and services project will cater for families from existing slum areas where population densities are high and environmental conditions are very bad. The project involves no slum clearance except for minimal relocation of overspill families. Three sites have been selected to provide 15,000 serviced plots under phase I of KUDP. The serviced plots for the EWS will be provided on a full cost recovery basis through a differential land pricing system. Gujaini site is one of the three sites.

(III) Agency Roles in Project Design and Implementation

The Kanpur Urban Development Project is sponsored by the state government of Uttar Pradesh. Financial assistance was received from the World Bank for the sites and services component.

To facilitate decision making in project development the KDA prepared an 'approach document' identifying the various problems regarding housing, environmental sanitation, small-scale enterprises, traffic, and transportation. World Bank missions helped in identifying the most essential components to be taken up on a priority basis. Thereafter a preliminary project was proposed at Gujaini site with full community participation to stimulate self help on the part of beneficiaries. Community participation has been seen as of prime importance from the planning to the implementation stage. UNICEF is supporting the project's community development component.

The KDA is the overall coordinating authority for phase I of the KUDP. In so far as the sites and services component is concerned, it is responsible for site selection, project planning, core house design and construction, and estate management. The Kanpur Nagar Mahapalika (KNM), the authority for drainage and sewerage, and Kanpur Jal Sansthan (KJS), the water supply authority, are together responsible for the planning and construction of project infrastructure and its maintenance.

The Project Formulation and Evaluation Unit, specially set up in the KDA, has completed the design and cost estimates of the 15,000 serviced plots at the three sites, Gujaini, Barra, and Pokhapur. The total cost of the sites and services component amounts to US$26.05 million, with the Gujaini project accounting for US$8.1 million.

The completion of the sites and services component is scheduled to take 3 years (1981–1984). In the first phase (1981–1982) land improvement, the construction of infrastructure (off-site and on-site), and on-plot development of the Gujaini site is being carried out. The Gujaini site covers an area of 74.3 hectares and will provide, 5,658 serviced plots.

The designing of, estimating, and tendering of land improvement was completed by March 1981 and execution would take 4.5 months. The construction of infrastructure (off-site and on-site) like roads, footpaths, drainage, sewerage, water supply, and street lighting, would take 3 to 9 months.

The construction of dwelling units was to be completed by the end of 1981. The construction of public facilities like schools, health centres, a police station, and community centres was to be carried out by June 1982.

Execution of infrastructure and construction works is being done through approved contractors. The project layout had been divided into matrix units. Each contractor is allotted all the on-site infrastructure and on-plot development work for one matrix. On the periphery of the matrices, various on-site/off-site infrastructure works like water storage tanks, sewerage, and roads are allotted to different contractors. Supply of controlled items like cement is arranged by the KDA. It has also been the practice of the KDA to supply steel to the contractors, but contractors have to arrange for the supply of the other materials.

(IV) The Target Group

The target population for the sites and services component are households with incomes between the 15th and 42nd percentiles of the Kanpur urban income distribution curve. The project is focused on the EWS group having household of incomes up to US$44 per month. Socio-economic surveys of the slums from where the majority of beneficiaries would be recruited revealed that about 80 per cent of households have monthly incomes up to US$55 per month. About 80 per cent of the population are illiterate while 14 per cent are only educated up to primary level.

The majority of households (74 per cent) pay rent whereas only 9 per cent occupy their own land. Some 12 per cent are squatters who pay no rent. Of the renters, 40 per cent pay monthly rents of less than US$1.00.

Health and environmental conditions are poor. The incidence of water-borne diseases is high. A 1979 survey revealed that 49 per cent of households used community latrines but a large number, 34 per cent, defecated in open drains or water courses. Water supply is also a problem. Whilst 53 per cent of the households take water from the community stand-pipes, other households used more dangerous sources such as wells which were often contaminated by their close proximity to cesspools, primitive pit latrines, and water courses.

Recruitment of project participants was carried out in January 1981 before infrastructural development and on-plot construction had been undertaken. Actual allotment will be done at the end of 1981.

(V) Land Selection and Acquisition

Site selection was based on the following criteria:

1 Consistency with Kanpur Master Plan land use.
2 Linkages with central city area.
3 Proximity to employment centres.
4 Quality of transportation available.
5 Physiography.

The 74.3 hectare Gujaini site, acquired by the KDA for US$12,500 per gross hectare, is within 3.5 km of the city centre and is in close proximity to existing industries and ongoing housing schemes. Gujaini site is well connected to the Kanpur city circulating network on the north-east side by an 18 m wide existing road and, on the south side, by a 60 m wide state highway (Lucknow by-pass). The main railway station of central Kanpur is 6 km away and the suburban station, Govindpuri, is about 3 km away.

The land of the vacant site slopes gently towards the Pandu River in the south and is crossed by two of its tributary canals. However, the site is fairly high and is not liable to flooding. The bearing capacity of the soil is 10 t/m^2. Being fairly level it requires no fills and cuts and the average cost of land improvement is marginal, amounting to US$2,800 per gross hectare. There are already ongoing housing schemes on the north side where off-site infrastructure is available.

(VI) Infrastructural Development Standards

Major roads for the Gujaini site will be either 18 m or 12 m in width. The 18 m road will form the bus route through the site. The roads are to be developed incrementally in terms of the quality (thickness) of the bitumen surface and the widths of the carriageways. Initially, carriageways for 18 m and 12 m major roads will be 3.7 m in width. Subsequently they will be widened by another 3.4 m when all the project plots are occupied. All nearby existing roads off-site will be connected with the project road network. Secondary roads will be either 7.5 or 6 m in width and tertiary roads (pedestrian walkways and cycle tracks) are either 4.5 or 3.5 m in width.

Water supply for the project will be drawn from two deep tube-wells with an expected discharge of 4.5 million litres per day. Around the clock supply will be possible through the utilization of a reservoir. As it is filtered water, only chlorination treatment will be required. The system has been designed to supply to the project population 150 litres per person per day.

All plots receive individual connections and, except for EWS plots, individual water metres. For the EWS plots there will be one communal metre for each 34 individual connections.

KDA will construct the water supply distribution system, tube-wells and treatment works, but KJS will maintain them. Eventually, the project water supply network will be connected to the city water supply so it will become a part of Kanpur water supply network.

The project sewerage system is designed for water consumption of 150 litres per capita, peak factor 3 and minimum velocity 0.8 m/s. RCC Humepipes of 150 to 700 millimetre diameter are to be used and a pumping station will be provided. The sewage will be discharged into an oxidation pond for primary treatment, then to a sewage farm and finally to the River Pandu.

Open drains have been provided on all roads and pedestrian footways. All surface drains will be connected to existing stormwater drains which will finally discharge into the River Pandu.

Kanpur city electricity generation and distribution is the responsibility of Kanpur Electricity Supply Administration (KESA). Electricity supply is available near Gujaini project site and six transformers of 630 kVA will be provided to service the project needs. The construction of the distribution network will be done by KESA. Street lights will be provided at 50-metre intervals on each electric pole. All the poles will be able to provide power connections. The payment collection and maintenance will be undertaken by KESA. The individual household supply will be metered, and the charges will be paid directly to KESA by the plot holders.

All standards applied in the project are in accordance with the norms of the relevant state authorities.

Garbage will be collected manually and carried to rubbish depots in handcarts and finally transported to a compost plant.

A bus service is available within a distance of 1 kilometre and it will be extended into the project area through the provision of two bus stops within a walking distance of 500 metres of every household.

Sufficient land has been set aside for primary schools and high schools to meet the project population's long-term needs. In the meantime, classrooms will be provided. Land has also been made available for other social facilities including health centres, a police station, a post office, and a community centre.

Public facilities like education and health care will be provided by the appropriate department of the state government in cooperation with the KDA within the project implementation period 1981–1984.

The standards for community facilities are based on the draft by-laws prepared by the committee instituted by the state government to implement the National Building Code.

(VII) Land Use

In the Gujaini project, 65.32 per cent of the total land will be marketed. This is substantially higher than in general housing schemes being prepared by other agencies. It will enable the KDA to assist the poorer target group by bringing down prices to affordable levels through adopting a differential land pricing system.

The land to be used for housing plots amounts to 49.10 per cent of the total site area. Commercial and industrial areas constitute 2.37 per cent and 1.79 per cent respectively. Community facilities account for 12.06 per cent, circulation for 24.61 per cent and open spaces 10.07 per cent (see Table 6, p.67).

All the standards pertaining to land use, plot size, building, and width of roads, etc., have been applied according to norms of the Indian Standards Institute (ISI) for low-cost housing. These standards do allow slight variations but are not in violation of the master plan land use provision.

(VIII) Dwelling Options, Allocation, and Repayment Arrangements

Some 68.72 per cent of the plots will be provided for the EWS category whose incomes range from US$25 to 44. Another 19.33 per cent of plots will be provided for the Low Income Group (LIG) whose incomes range from US$50 to 75. The remaining plots will be provided for Middle and Higher Income Groups, the latter having income over US$200 per month.

The core options are designed for the possibility of vertical expansion, ultimately providing two rooms. Indigenous building materials like lime, brick powder and fly ash will be used in construction with a minimum amount of cement and steel. The plot area of 36.75 m^2 is the same for the four options designed for the EWS.

Option I includes a sanitary core of 1.4 m^2 with a 1.22 m high wall. To enable him to construct his shelter the plot holder will be eligible for a materials loan of US$188. This option will be marketed to households with monthly incomes of up to US$25. The monthly payment will be US$2.25 for the unit and US$1.80 for the materials loan.

Option II will be provided with the sanitary core, a 23 cm thick common courtyard wall and all walls for the eventual two rooms. The occupant will initially erect a thatched roof to provide a total built area of 21.28 m^2. The household can get a US$125 construction materials loan to complete their shelter. The monthly payment for this unit will be US$4.75 and US$1.20 for the materials loan. This unit is being marketed to households in the income range US$25.00–32.50 per month.

Option III will be the same as option II but will be fitted with an RCC roof and a WC. It will be marketed to households with monthly incomes of US$32.50–37.50 per month. Provision will be made for 50 per cent of the households to take up a materials loan of US$125. The monthly repayment without the materials loan will be US$6.75 per month.

Option IV is a developed form of option III and comes complete with doors, shutters for the room, and WC. Addressed to income groups of US$37.50–43.75 per month, it requires repayments of US$9.70 per month. Again, provision of a US$125.00 materials loan for 50 per cent of the families will be made available.

The KDA plans to give materials loans (for cement, bricks, and steel) to the plot holders according to the option requirement. It is proposed that residents will utilize the materials given to them within one month, with self help and with the help of a local contractor. It is proposed that the KDA will give free technical assistance. A site office of the KDA will be provided at Gujaini site to give such guidance.

An occupant can complete the dwelling unit with both new and second-hand materials and there is no restriction. Standard plans of various options will be provided to allottees for the extension of their shelter. Financial help for extension may be made available through banks.

All land belonging to the government is allotted on a leasehold basis, usually for 90 years, and the same policy has been adopted for this project. Therefore, the plots will be provided on a leasehold basis, initially for 30 years, with provision for their renewal up to 90 years subject to rent increases of 50 per cent every 30 years. The plots will be allotted to families on the basis of household income and on the condition that the family does not own a house or a plot in Kanpur urban area. The rules and regulations for allocation, registration, sale, resale, subletting, change of use, mortgage, etc., are the same as for other national housing schemes though they will be reviewed in the hope of making them less complicated for the allottees.

Though the target population will depend for regular employment on the existing employment centres, provision has been made for permitting household industries to augment the household incomes of the plot holders. It is also proposed to provide business loans for small-scale entrepreneurs to enable them to increase their household incomes.

(IX) Financial Arrangements

The Planning Commission of the Government of India and the Planning Department of the State of Uttar Pradesh decide the priorities of various sectors. This forms the basis for the planned allocation of budgets, both in the states and centrally in the regular national budgets. Market borrowings are permitted with the prior approval of the Reserve Bank of India within the limits of planned allocations.

The current policy is to subsidize the cost of the land to be allotted to the economically weaker sections of society. To achieve this, a differential land pricing pattern has been adopted that enables cross-subsidization. Residential serviced plots for EWS have been subsidized to the extent of 55 per cent. The bigger the plot size (with a better standard of infrastructure), the higher the land price. Prices for residential plots range from US$4 to 6 per square metre, and for industrial and commercial plots US$25 per square metre. Land for community facilities like schools, health centres, police stations and post offices is priced at 50 per cent of the actual developed land cost.

Beneficiaries, after finalizing the agreement with KDA, will be given possession of the land and the dwelling unit on it. The instalments payable by them according to the agreement are to be paid to the KDA collection centre. The Estate Department of the KDA will keep the accounts of such payments. In case of default, beneficiaries will have to pay penalty interest together with the instalment due.

Chapter 3

Agencies and Sites and Services Projects

3.1 National Policy and the Implementing Agency

In Chapter 1 it was noted that the adoption of slum upgrading and sites and services into national housing policies came as a result of political and economic expedience and not out of conviction. Government officials and politicians of many developing countries, who were involved in the formulation of national housing policy, perceived that existing public construction programmes were not yielding results on the needed scale and proved too expensive, necessitating considerable subsidies. At the same time, foreign aid institutions like the World Bank changed their lending policies in the field of housing to supporting slum upgrading and sites and services strategies rather than conventional housing. Consequently, local housing authorities were inclined to shift to slum upgrading and sites and services activities. However, it is important to keep in mind the fact that the policy makers themselves and the professionals working in the housing agencies were not really comfortable with such policy shifts and the new roles they implied: slum upgrading and sites and services are essentially still regarded as second-best options, only acceptable because of the force of circumstances.

The sites and services strategy has been difficult for many housing professionals to accept because its efficient operation requires changes in the traditional operational structure of their agencies and the nature of their professional roles. In particular, the dominant roles of the architects and engineers in these institutions are necessarily modified and reduced to allow greater participation by other professionals from other disciplines such as economics and sociology. Moreover, the management of sites and services project development is very different from the conventional housing agency task of centralized construction. It calls for the participation of the incoming residents in house design and construction (in varying degrees) and for considerable reductions in design and construction standards. Consequently, architects and engineers feel that they are being called upon to do the very opposite of what their professional associations are urging them to do. In sites and services schemes they are asked to use minimal standards rather than higher standards. They are asked to build less of the house (in some options none at all) and leave the bulk of the construction for the families to organize themselves.

Apart from these understandable professional reservations about the desirability and viability of sites and services, less scrupulous housing agency bureaucrats are reluctant to see conventional housing projects replaced by sites and services schemes because the latter provide fewer opportunities for graft, perquisites and because of outside pressures from the construction industry.

Sites and services schemes are complex and problematic in their social, economic and financial structure. The kind of comprehensive analyses and monitoring required in the design and implementation of sites and services projects makes heavy demands on an agency's scarce appropriate specialist personnel. Such appropriate specialists, even when they are available, may also have difficulty fitting into institutions which formerly have only allotted them marginal roles. The particular biases of disciplines as traditionally remote as, for example, engineering and sociology, are not easily overcome and often result in uncooperative attitudes that make a multidisciplinary housing strategy like sites and services even more difficult than it already is.

It is also worth noting that sites and services projects and slum upgrading schemes have expanded the range of items dealt with by housing authorities. The addition of a range of new social services such as education, employment and nutrition programmes has entailed more unfamiliar organizational and coordinating roles for housing agencies. It has also caused difficulties in project design and has raised management costs.

The assimilation of what we may at present believe to be better policies by local housing agencies has also led to some 'image' problems. Partly this is the result of the different social and political emphasis of the policy itself. The tendency to direct public aid and institutional support primarily to the poor is ethically laudable, but often it is politically novel and questioned by other, more powerful, interest groups. Even while the more enlightened politicians and officials may see benefits in increased social equity, many others do not.

Another cause of such 'image' problems is probably already clear from the earlier chapters: i.e. the move to spread public resources by facilitating more habitat improvement and housing opportunities for larger numbers of economically disadvantaged families leads to slow, gradual housing development. Sites and services projects are carried out over a longer period of time largely because of the families' need to complete their houses gradually. Gradual, individual family extensions of core houses also do not look as tidy as uniformly built conventional housing units. For these reasons, sites and services do not have an efficient image even though they may actually be far more efficient by strict economic criteria than conventional public housing programmes. However, when implementing agencies do not adhere to the austere spirit of the strategy and invest too heavily in infrastructure and core house construction, their projects' efficiency and effectiveness are seriously impaired. This, of course, tends to reinforce the negative attitude of those architects and engineers who consider the approach as misguided and inappropriate anyway.

3.2 Project Goals, Agency Structure, and Community Participation

Many sites and services proejcts run into serious problems because government housing agencies are often insufficiently attuned to the various planning and implementation processes essential for project success. In many cases, housing agencies have done little to identify what structural organizational modifications are necessary to enable them successfully to design, implement and manage this particular type of project. Inability or unwillingness to recognize and remedy organizational deficiencies has led to much confusion, inefficiency and a movement away from the actual strategy itself. Thus, too often, the provision of basic serviced plots is not the main focus of project design and delivery. Rather there is a preoccupation with core house design and prescriptive controls on its development and extension as well as with high standards of site planning and infrastructure, both of which reflect conventional organizational and professional biases in the agencies.

The important facilitating strategy of involving the target community in the design and implementation, despite the stress that it receives in feasibility studies and project formulation documents, is only partially achieved at best in most agencies. Effective community involvement has seldom been achieved, partly because of the structural inflexibility of the agency and partly because of the inappropriateness of their personnel.

The failure of most government designed and implemented sites and services projects to provide for the involvement of target communities and populations in appropriate areas constitutes a clear divergence from the sites and services concept. The strategy of providing minimum plots (possibly with core housing) and minimum but gradually upgradable infrastructure is only feasible if the households involved in the project are cooperating in depth with the project organizers to achieve the project's goals. The stimulus and catalyst for this fairly long-term cooperation is the householders' understanding of and satisfaction with what the project offers them. Such understanding and satisfaction can only be achieved by allowing them to participate in decisions on the design, implementation, and management of the project. Actually, very little effort has gone into finding out how to get popular inputs into sites and services projects. Agencies generally justify this by claiming that they do not have the appropriate staff to do this, or that it would slow down project implementation.

Admittedly, staff trained and with experience to deal appropriately with community participation are not readily available in the majority of housing bureaucracies. However, there are encouraging developments in institutions which have gained substantial experience with self help housing, such as, for example, the Habitat Hyderabad Project Wing of the Hyderabad Municipal Courporation, India. The conversion of conventional housing agency staff (architects, engineers, etc.) to new professional roles cannot be done overnight. It is not merely a matter of professional training either. A significant shift in attitude is required, especially because the inculcation of community participation into project design and implementation implies the sharing of responsibility and authority. The sharing of the latter is unfamiliar (and a little threatening) to the traditional bureaucratic mentality, but it is necessary if the agencies concerned seriously want to make the sites and services approach work. It is the only way in which they can hand over a large part of the task of shelter provision and community management to the people and thereby free themselves to concentrate on broader access and facilitating activities (such as land provision, services provision, employment development, and access to finance) that support the community in its tasks.

The common agency plea that people's participation in design and in decision making during project implementation will slow down its execution is to a large degree true. Generally, agencies are under pressure to complete project design and get projects implemented rapidly. This pressure is mostly political in nature, but is also exerted by funding agencies. However, if project staff have not taken the time necessary to enlist the residents' support and cooperation, then more serious problems can be expected later on, such as large-scale defaults on repayments. Sites and services projects cannot normally be executed in as short a time as conventional housing projects or slum upgrading projects.* Therefore, lending institutions should take this into account from the outset and encourage implementing agencies to take time to involve the people as much as possible in the carrying out of the project. Even though the resulting delays will lead to increases in construction costs and funds being tied up for a longer period of time (higher interest costs) both resulting in higher repayment burdens for families or in subsidies, they should be regarded as the lesser evil and therefore necessary.

Certainly many government agencies can reasonably plead that their inexperience is a major obstacle to their effective involvement of would-be communities in their projects. But there is a need to be willing to learn from more experienced organizations elsewhere. All the mistakes do not have to be made in every context. Willingness to learn from other organizations with longer experience and better performance records is vital to the development of better projects in their own context. One such organization is the World Bank supported El Salvador Foundation of Development and Minimum Housing, a small non-profit making foundation that was very successful in its sites and services type projects in the 1970s. Its practice of involving the project participants in mutual-aid project construction and in some decision making yielded very positive results in terms of self-reliant communities and successful cost recovery records. The history of this organization also demonstrates that experience in successive projects helps to develop simple practical techniques for involving would-be participants in the design stage of sites and services projects. By taking its incoming householders to earlier project sites, it is able to get feedback on what their preferences and needs

---

* The difference in this regard with slum upgrading projects is generally caused by differences in project size, and by the fact that dealing with an existing community in an existing location is normally easier.

are so these can be incorporated in the design of the next project.

Other less comprehensive methods of getting the people's inputs into project design and implementation exist and have been explored in many places. These include demonstration projects and the construction of prototype houses. All these methods are essentially similar to those which private sector housing developers employ to develop products that are more attractive to home buyers. The fact that such methods are often not employed in public sector housing is indicative of the public sector's attitude towards its so-called 'beneficiaries'.

A major drawback to government housing agency performance derives from the fact that such agencies are not in normal competition with other organizations or companies doing or producing the same kind of project or product, so they are not disciplined by real market conditions. Two serious consequences are that there is little knowledge or understanding of the market and little impetus to develop an efficient organization and procedures to execute projects. Project design is seldom guided by the real economic tensions between the agency's financial resources and what it is to produce; between the real needs of the client and the acceptability to the client of what he is being sold; between the way in which the product is being produced and the organization and staff that produces it. Various sites and services projects have suffered anomalies and mismatches as a result.

In the Metroville I project in Karachi, for example, non-occupation of allotted plots persisted over several years. This was a direct result of a lack of understanding of the prevailing land and housing market, together with a lack of coordination between the Master Plan Department of the Karachi Development Authority (KDA), responsible for planning the scheme, and the KDA's implementing department. Not only had plots been allocated largely to home owning middle-class people instead of to the low income families for whom they were intended but, over and above this, a water supply would not be provided for the well-situated project area for several years to come.

In order to avoid such mistakes, serious market research is required. In this respect the initiatives taken by the Madras Metropolitan Development Authority (MMDA) are worth mentioning. Having confronted the initially limited success it achieved in the Arumbakkam project, the MMDA has embarked upon pre-project marketing for its next scheme. This takes the form of advance promotion (advertising) of the scheme in leaflets and newspapers, on radio and television, allowing a longer period of time for interested families to respond, and actually taking groups of families to visit the site of its implementing scheme at Arumbakkam in order to gain inputs from the people on design issues.

3.3 Agency Roles and Interagency Coordination

All of the projects reviewed at the seminar involve several government agencies in the course of their implemention. Usually one agency (a national housing authority or metropolitan development authority) has the major responsibility for the project with other agencies supplying inputs from their respective fields of activity. Two basic models of project management can be discerned.

The first is the highly centralized or integrative model involving one agency that designs, implements, and manages the sites and services project with only the funding and one or two services, like water supply or electricity, coming from other agencies. The Dakshinpuri scheme in Delhi, India, and the Tung Song Hong project in Bangkok, Thailand, are examples of this approach.

The second model is a cooperative one that involves a wide range of government and other agencies in particular project components. These are coordinated by an agency which is usually responsible for project design and subsequently for coordinating its implementation and estate management. The Arumbakkam scheme in Madras is an example of this type.

Although the first model seems to have produced sites and services projects more rapidly than the second, it has clear disadvantages. It necessitates a concentration of skilled and experienced manpower in the agency that cannot usually be achieved. As a result, quite serious mistakes can be made without being noticed until too late. If the cooperative model is being employed, then the range of specialist skills is more likely to be available within the various agencies involved, and their collective vigilance is more able to pick up errors and weaknesses in time to correct or overcome them. On the other hand, there are problems in achieving cooperation and goodwill between agencies which will be considered below.

Another problem with the first model is that it is too centralized for the kind of tasks that sites and services schemes should be concentrating on, namely those supporting the income residents. In this sense there is a conflict of roles because, if the agency is designing, implementing, and managing the project, it is likely to assume the image of landlord and debt collector, and this will not facilitate its efforts to win the trust and cooperation of the community in order to build community self-reliance. The distribution or separation of roles that takes place in the second model avoids this conflict and opens up the community to a more natural variety of influences and assistance.

Perhaps the most serious weakness of the integrative model is that it creates too much of a united front of administrators and experts vis-à-vis the community residents. It is too powerful and therefore less likely to be responsive to individual and community needs and wishes. When various roles are spread among several agencies, including, hopefully, some non-government agencies, there is more opportunity for residents to air their grievances and get their point across through the advocacy of one of the agencies involved. (This, of course, unfortunately assumes that the community has been given little power in executive decision making.)

The cooperative model has by no means been perfected in the Asian project experiences to date. Some projects seem to have been quite difficult to coordinate, partly because of the number of agencies involved and partly because of the nature of these agencies themselves.

Coordination problems are often important obstacles to successful sites and services project development. They are not impossible to overcome but require a well-coordinated planning effort right from the outset. The Arumbakkam project in Madras demonstrates that if there is sufficient goodwill and understanding of each organization's role, effective projects can be developed. In this case, most of the agencies concerned were consulted in planning decisions, most notably the Madras Corporation and the Tamil Nadu Housing Board, both of which were involved in implementation. Other agencies brought in at an early stage were the Small Industries Development Corporation, nationalized banks, cooperatives, and voluntary agencies concerned with community development.

The fact that the model is a communicative one, involving continuous dialogue between the agencies over a period of time, suggests that it is a better match to the sites and services project task. It can more easily foster community groups to develop and participate in what is already a bargaining session between the different parties.

The experience of the Calcutta Metropolitan Development Authority (CMDA) is pertinent to this discussion. The CMDA had initially used the cooperative model in the design, implementation, and management of its projects in much the same way as the MMDA has in its Arumbakkam project. However, the CMDA had considerable difficulty in soliciting and coordinating the cooperation of other authorities and agencies, so it changed over to the centralized model for its Baishnabghata-Patuli Area Development Project in the hope that, if it carried out all the activities itself, it could expedite the project and carry it out with greater efficiency. More recently, CMDA staff have found that such a change has not been as beneficial as expected. Undertaking all the roles of planning, funding, implementing, managing, and recovering repayments has placed too great a burden on the authority's resources. As a result there is a move to return some functions to other agencies and to leave the authority itself more freedom to co-ordinate overall activities and to carry out components — like project design, the selection of participants, and the allocation of plots — which it can do well.

The implications here are that the context itself plays an important part in deciding how best to approach a project. It should be noted that in some contexts the local agencies that might normally be included in the project task are not able or willing to support the coordinating agency. Therefore, it is not possible to lay down any hard and fast rules on the matter. All that can be said is that, all things being equal, the cooperative model does seem to be a more open one (and would more readily admit the participation of non-government agencies) and it is therefore also more attuned to the sites and services approach. In the integrative or centralized model the agency concerned is likely to become overburdened with responsibilities, which in turn may lead to less flexible procedures and a less responsive attitude to the public it is supposed to be serving.

3.4 Case Study Focus

The case study considered below, the Dakshinpuri Resettlement Scheme in New Delhi, is an example of the integrative model discussed above. It was designed and implemented by the Delhi Development Authority (DDA) with funding from the Housing and Urban Development Corporation (HUDCO).

Case Study IV DAKSHINPURI RESETTLEMENT SCHEME, DELHI

(1) Background

In terms of the scale of needs and scarcity of resources for housing, few countries confront the challenge that India does. With an estimated backlog of some 20 million dwelling units in the nation as a whole (Housing and Urban Development Corporation, 1978, p.5) the urgency of the problem has stimulated resourcefulness and political will to find solutions that hold promise for meeting present and future needs. At national and state levels, policy and legislative initiatives have been taken to ensure the availability of urban land and loan finance for the provision of improved environmental conditions, shelter and employment for low income people.

Legislation limiting land ownership has been of particular importance in gaining government access to land at non-speculative prices. This is especially the case in large urban centres like Delhi, Calcutta and Bombay.* Legislation coopting the participation of private sector banks in lending for low income housing has also been instrumental in allowing a coordinated and realistic national programme of human settlements to get underway. At the national level, the Housing and Urban Development Corporation Ltd (HUDCO), a central government enterprise, has been of great significance in directing loans and funding to urban housing projects in every state of the nation. From its creation in 1970 until 1978 it sanctioned loans totalling Rs32,783 million for the constructive of 322,349 houses and 4,543 non-residential buildings and the development of 47,243 plots in 17 states and 4 union territories. The 2.5 million beneficiaries, of whom 88 per cent were from the lowest income group (economically weaker section), lived in 775 cities and towns.

Within this general context we can review the policies operating in relation to the city of Delhi's slum upgrading and sites and services programme and, at the same time, look to the Dakshinpuri Resettlement Scheme as a representative result of such policies.

The population of Delhi increased from 2.36 million in 1961 to 5.42 in 1980. By the year 2001 it is expected to reach 12 million. The income distribution of

* However, state governments and government enterprises do not always use such progressive legislation to the advantage of the poor; in fact, often such agencies operate very much in the way a real estate developer would. See Sarin (1982) for examples of this from Bombay and Delhi.

Delhi's households shows that 73 per cent earn less than US$80 per month, and clearly their ability to pay for improved services and housing is very low.

A large-scale land acquisition, development, and disposal policy was adopted to ensure a supply of land when appropriate and at a reasonable price to safeguard the interests of the poor. The land disposal policy is aimed at allocating developed land to various income groups in the following proportions: 50 per cent to the economically weaker section (EWS) and low income group (LIG), 30 per cent to middle income group (MIG), 20 per cent to the higher income group (HIG). The developed land is provided for the various income groups on long-term lease, with the lease premium equivalent to the cost of the land plus a marginal profit. However, in the case of the relocation of squatters who had been squatting since before 1960, the cost of land development is subsidized to the extent of 50 per cent.

The Delhi Development Authority (DDA) has been undertaking housing action through direct construction, environmental improvement programmes and sites and services schemes. The latter have now resettled more than 200,000 families, some of whom, however, were forcibly evicted by the DDA from more valuable central city locations during the emergency period 1975–1977* The Dakshinpuri project is typical of the sites and services resettlement projects carried out by the DDA.

(II) Site Selection, Acquisition, and Development

The project aimed to house and resettle squatter families on the 78.6 hectare Dakshinpuri site on the main Mehrauli-Badarpur Road within a 5 kilometre radius of various employment centres. The land had been acquired because of its good location, and because it was virtually vacant and not subject to flooding. The land was acquired by the Delhi administration for US$1.30 per square metre in 1975 and turned over to the DDA. The DDA was the sole actor for the physical, social, and economic development of the project. It developed the land, designed and implemented the project, and provided, or arranged for the provision of, the necessary services. The central government decided on the policies concerning physical and economic requirements. It also stipulated ceiling costs of the plots and core housing, and accordingly released money to the DDA for project implementation. The project design was completed by August 1975 and, on acquiring the land, the DDA engaged contractors to level the site. Survey work was carried out, and subsequently the land development work and the construction of core houses were undertaken by contractors. Essential construction materials like cement and steel were made available to the contractors by the DDA.

---

* See Sarin (1982) for a description of the rationale for and methods used in the eviction of the squatters by DDA during this period.

(III) The Target Groups

The sites and services resettlement programme at Dakshinpuri and its extension was aimed at squatter families scattered in some 1,400 squatter areas all over Delhi. The estimated 150,000 families involved live in appalling conditions, deprived of basic utilities, services and facilities. Surveys in 1973–1977 revealed that 71 per cent of the families had monthly incomes of less than US$33.50 and 24 per cent had incomes between US$33.50 and US$60.00. For purposes of recruitment to the project the squatters were divided into two categories: those who had been squatters prior to 1960 were categorized as 'eligible' and those who had commenced squatting after that date as 'ineligible'. In fact, the scheme was able to provide plots and improved environmental conditions for a total of 13,161 families from both categories.

(IV) Land Use and Infrastructural Standards

The Dakshinpuri site is very well connected to the urban road network of Delhi. The circulation system within the project consists of 24 m wide main roads which run through the site. The secondary roads, which are either 18 m or 13.5 m in width, feed into the main road system and provide access to the residential areas. The residential clusters are served by 9 m wide streets and 5 m pathways. All the roads are surfaced and ultimately will be developed to the standards and designs prescribed by the Town and County Planning Organization. The road system within the site, though actually built by the DDA, will be turned over the municipal corporation for maintenance.

The water supply for the community is being drawn from four tube-wells which connect with an underground reservoir of 0.7 million litres capacity. An overhead tank of 0.45 million litres, with a staging height of 27.5 m, is used to store water pumped from the wells and to distribute it to Dakshinpuri site. On the south side of the site two surface reservoirs of 0.56 million and 1.13 million litres respectively have been constructed, and these connect to four other tube-wells, enabling supply to the Dakshinpuri extension. More recently, two additional tube-wells, each of 45,000 litres per hour capacity, were constructed to provide a 50 per cent increase in water supply capacity. An adequate number of automatic chlorinators have been provided in the tube-wells and reservoirs. It is intended to supply individual water connections to households in the near future.

The area has not been provided with a separate water-borne sewerage system because there is no trunk sewer facility in the vicinity. Instead, communal toilet blocks have been provided that utilize 80 m^3 capacity septic tanks.

The electricity supply to Dakshinpuri is through seven substations each having a capacity of 650 kVA. These substations are constructed on plots of 13.8 × 18.5 m each. The substations get their supply from the Indraprastha power station which is controlled by Delhi Electricity Supply Undertaking (DESU). This supply is through overhead wires supported on prestressed concrete poles placed at 30 metres c/c. The project ultimately aims at supplying electricity to individual plots.

It should be remembered that though the infrastructural design standards applied are minimal, they are better than the people had enjoyed in the squatter settlements. Furthermore, they are designed to be upgraded over time in accordance with the people's ability to pay.

Community facilities like schools, open spaces, shops, and health and recreation centres were provided at the standard approved by the competent authority. Besides providing nursery, primary and secondary schools, shopping and health facilities and adult literacy centres were constructed. Industrial training centres and child welfare centres were also provided in the scheme. Two such child welfare centres, two industrial training centres, and five adult education centres are functioning. The site offers convenient shopping in 22 fair price shops (selling at governmentally approved prices) and a super bazaar (a government run departmental store).

The Delhi Transport Corporation (DTC) provides public transportation for the residents. Around 20 bus routes ply this area and the buses are available at 20-minute intervals. The major modes of transport are by bus and cycle.

Garbage is collected from refuse receptacles provided at suitable locations.

The overall land use distribution in the project is as follows: residential — 32.60 per cent; circulation — 24.85 per cent; facilities — 20.21 per cent; parks and playgrounds — 16.27 per cent; commercial — 5.92 per cent; other uses — 0.17 per cent (see Table 6, p.67).

(V) Allocation, Rental Conditions, and House Development

Under the initial plot size and disposal policy the cost of each 70 m^2 plot was to be subsidized to the extent of 50 per cent, the balance being given as a loan to be recovered in monthly instalments of US$1.40 over 10 years. The ceiling cost fixed for such a 70 m^2 plot was to be US$733.30. However, plot size was changed to 20.9 m^2 in view of the fact that such a price would be beyond what the families targeted for this project could afford, and because project designers realized that such a large plot seriously restricted the number of families that could be accommodated on the site. In contrast, 20.9 m^2 plot provided a general improvement in terms of space for the vast majority of squatter families in comparison with their accommodation in the squatter areas, and enabled the project to absorb a far greater number of families.

In this squatter resettlement project the plots were given to the dwellers on leasehold for an undefined period as they were considered as camping sites. In the initial stages the plots were given on a leasehold basis with a ban on transfer or sale. The monthly rents are different for 'eligible' squatters (prior to 1960) and 'ineligible' squatters. Eligible squatters have to pay a rent of US$0.46 per m^2 on the basis of 50 per cent subsidy as compared with ineligible squatters who pay US$0.90 per m^2. In both cases an additional amount of

US$0.13 per m^2 is charged for water and conservancy services. As the plots were given on a rental basis there was no title registration.

Families who had been allocated plots initially were brought to the site even though the infrastructural development work had not commenced. They were initially accommodated in tents, temporary toilet blocks were constructed, and water supply arrangements were made to meet their needs whilst infrastructural work was in progress.

Later, the project provided permanent community latrines and a community water supply. The construction of shelter was left to the individual families according to their needs and resources. Various types of building materials from very temporary to very good quality were utilized by residents. In most cases the original shelter constructed on-site by the residents has been gradually improved since the project began. The people have arranged their own finance through their own contacts.

Although, under state building regulations, permanent house construction would not be permitted on a 20.9 m^2 plot, the DDA is allowing such construction in accordance with a standard design prepared for the guidance of the people. This is a two-storeyed structure which allows for incremental development. The floor coverage allowed is 100 per cent on the ground floor and 75 per cent (16.50 m^2) on the first floor. Thus, in the final stage a plot holder can achieve a house of 37–41 m^2 floor area. A cluster for 2,500 persons was used as a basic planning unit consisting of at least 500 household plots and supplied with facilities like communal toilet blocks and three or four shops. Each cluster is generally bounded by a 9 to 13.5 m wide metalled road with a 5 m wide pedestrian way through the cluster itself. For every two clusters a primary school and larger shopping facilities are provided. Every four clusters have a secondary school and other facilities provided.

Upon the occupation of the dwelling plots civic amenities such as post and telegraphic services were provided by the relevant state body. State funds supported the construction of schools, dispensaries, police and fire stations, and the public transportation system.

(VI) Socio-economic Conditions in the New Community

In 1976, the population of Dakshinpuri and the extension was around 65,800.*
They are predominantly Hindu (94.33 per cent) and mainly speak Hindi. Only 31 per cent of the population is literate. The average household size is five persons as compared with an average household size of eight in Madangir village which is near the project site.

The work force was primarily employed in the services sector (as watchmen, cleaners, gardeners and servants), as construction workers and in various informal entrepreneurial activities. The majority of those engaged in

* Survey conducted by the School of Planning and Architecture, New Delhi, in 1976, when the site was not yet fully occupied.

employment commuted more than 15 kilometres to their places of work. Some 44 per cent commuted by bicycle and 33 per cent use buses. In fact, community time and travel costs are major problems: places of employment are often close to the places where the families once lived.

Many of the settlers were still extremely poor. Some 68.2 per cent earned less than US$40 per month, 19.7 per cent earned between US$40.00 and 60.65 and only 12.1 per cent earned more than US$60.65. Various efforts are being undertaken to improve this situation by providing job-oriented training. The State Industrial Development Corporation runs a training centre in Dakshinpuri. Five adult literacy centres are functioning in this area. Some religious and charitable organizations are tackling the problem of employment and income generation for women. Some of the income generating activities are envelope making, selling vegetables, food processing, and sewing. There are also child welfare centres to care for the health and education of the children.

On the issue of resale, the project performance is very good. In 1980 an informal survey conducted by the DDA revealed that the number of units changing hands (albeit illegally) was negligible. A change in the tenure of plots was under consideration at the time of the seminar. Letting rooms of subletting the house occurred on some 40 per cent of the plots. Some 3 per cent of families have opened small shops on their premises. Both of these activities are tolerated by the DDA as they are sources of supplementary income for the households concerned.

Chapter 4

Implementing Sites and Services

4.1 Selection of Intended Settlers

The value of establishing (as thoroughly as possible within a particular context) who the target households are, before embarking on site selection and acquisition, is that it can enable their participation from the earliest stages in the location and design of the project. Although such identification and recruitment of the target group is more difficult than in slum upgrading projects, in so far as they would need to be identified prior to project design, it is none the less possible to some degree. Identifying the target group from the outset can help to establish more clearly what resources the people can bring to the project in terms of finance, housing materials, and building skills. Also, it can enable some involvement of the target group in project design which, although it requires considerable time, can ensure a better match between project design and target group priorities and preferences.

In general, the Asian projects reviewed are only based on a theoretical knowledge of their target population. No clarifying steps such as preselection of eligible householders took place till implementation of the project on the site was under way. Only two projects, the Dagat-Dagatan project in Manila and the Arumbakkam project in Madras, actually attempting any participation on the part of prospective residents in project design (even then, only at a basic level).

Of the 14 projects, only one, the Simomulyo resettlement project in Surabaya, Indonesia, was specifically designed to relocate an existing squatter community which had been identified prior to project design. Three other projects, the Dakshinpuri project in Delhi, the Baishnavghata-Patuli project in Calcutta, and the Dagat-Dagatan project in the Philippines, gave priority to relocatees from ongoing slum improvement projects in the respective cities.

In all but two projects, namely the Rangsit scheme in Bangkok and the Metroville I scheme in Karachi, strict income criteria are planned or applied in selecting project households. Usually these take the form of a set of stipulated income ranges, with the larger percentage of plots going to the lower income groups and a smaller percentage going to the middle and higher income groups (see Table 5). Needless to say, there are difficulties involved in establishing actual incomes, and the problem is exacerbated by some confusion about whether the income of the head of household alone should be counted, or whether collective household income would be more indicative of ability to pay. Attitudes differ on this issue from case to case.

Certainly some projects take far greater pains to screen out applicants who might have been slightly better off than the target groups originally decided upon. The NHA of the Philippines, for example, fairly successfully screens

Table 5 Income groups in reviewed projects (each group as percentage of total project households)

Project	Households below subsistence income	Households between subsistence and 2 × subsistence income	Households between 2 × subsistence income and 4 × subsistence income	Households 4 × subsistence income and over
Vashi, New Bombay	20.0	60.0	20.0	—
Rangsit, Bangkok	11.0	66.0	17.0	6.0
Tung Song Hong,[a] Bangkok	22.0	69.0	9.0	—
Bang Plee Bang Bor,[a] Bangkok	25.0	30.0	35.5	8.5
Dakshinpuri resettlement, Delhi	76.2	23.8	—	—
Arumbakkam, Madras	74.0	21.0	5.0	—
Baishnavghata-Patuli,[a] Calcutta	20.0	40.0	20.0	20.0
Dagat-Dagatan, Manila	20.0	50.0	20.0	10.0
Dasmariñas Bagong Bayan, Manila	25.0	60.0	15.0	—
Bekasi Perumnas project, Jakarta	27.0	20.0	23.0	30.0
Perumnas project, Medan	4.4	51.9	36.8	6.9
Simomulyo resettlement, Surabaya	2.5	77.2	17.3	3.0
Metroville I, Karachi	18.0	37.0	30.0	5.0
Gujaini sites and services,[a] Kanpur	68.0	20.0	11.0	1.0

[a] Targeted households only.

NB   There are two important limitations to this table: (1) the basic problem is defining subsistence income in a single context and comparing one context with another; (2) the data for several projects are not reliable. Therefore, it should only be taken as a rough guide to the economic level of actual project participants.

out 'affluent squatters' — those capable of fending for themselves — and admit only the very poor to their Dasmariñas sites and services scheme. In contrast, in its Rangsit project, the NHA of Thailand, having received few applications from its originally declared income range of US$75 per month or less, abandoned this criterion and subsequently invited applications from the Bangkok public generally.

To some extent the Bekasi Perumnas project in Jakarta and the Perumnas project in Medan are unique in so far as both mainly restricted recruitment to civil servants from certain categories. In the Medan project 75 per cent of the units were distributed to civil servants and retired civil servants and their surviving spouses and to military personnel (both active and retired) and their surviving spouses, and 25 per cent to employees of government enterprises and the private sector as well as to relocatees from other government programmes. In the Bekasi Perumnas project, eligible families had to have a minimum of five members and household heads had to be in government service at grades I or II. The Arumbakkam project in Madras allotted 10 per cent of its plots to low-level government employees and 20 per cent to scheduled castes and tribes.

A stipulation of all projects is that applicants cannot own any other land in the city except the plot they would be taking up in the sites and services scheme.

In open allocation projects (which are not geared to a specific existing slum community that is being evicted or relocated) it seems useful that group applications from stipulated income levels be given some priority, as members of such groups usually can be expected to be supportive to one another in the early, rather demoralizing years of the project. In practice, most of the projects reviewed had not done this. The Metroville I project in Karachi, however, had sought applications from groups of 20 families who were working in the industrial operations located near the site. In the Dakshinpuri scheme in Delhi the agency concerned, the Delhi Development Authority, is now considering recruitment of future sites and services households in groups set up by eligible families themselves.

Unfortunately, there has been a tendency to carry out selection somewhat late in the projects' development cycle, usually well after infrastructural development has been completed. In some Thai and Philippine projects wasteful delays occurred in the selection and allocation processes and many plots remained vacant for a considerable period. The causes are not always within the control of the project management. For example, in the Tung Song Hong project in Bangkok, the NHA of Thailand is involved in litigation with the contractor over escalation of costs and additional work, so it has cancelled its initial allocation of units to date because it does not want to keep the allottees waiting for a long time until the legal battle is over. One project, the Dakshinpuri resettlement in Delhi, did carry out allocation promptly and made arrangements for the families to come onto the site, even before the infrastructural work was under way.*

4.2 Site Selection and Land Acquisition

The Asian projects reviewed rely predominantly on publicly owned lands for project sites. The fact that eight projects out of fourteen used public land

* This was possible only due to the peculiar political circumstances at the time, which enabled DDA to evict squatters before proper relocation facilities were ready for occupation. See Sarin (1982) for a background to this emergency relocation.

suggests a tendency to exploit public lands before exploring the possibilities of acquiring privately owned land (mostly at market prices). This, coupled with the fact that, in all projects except one, project site land was under agricultural use or only sparsely occupied and utilized, indicates that project agencies are not eager to explore the viability of less remote and more attractive locations. Indeed, although for 13 out of 14 projects it was claimed that their sites were selected because of their good locations in terms of employment opportunities and access to service networks, more prominent reasons included free or low-cost land, easy acquisition, and few or no existing occupants of the land. In fact, the choice of poor-quality land in several projects necessitated expensive land improvement investment. This took the form of draining swampy lands and installing dyke and bund protection from flooding, or partial land fill in some projects and land levelling and landscaping in others.

Of all projects reviewed, ten sites follow the direction of urban growth. Five of the sites are within 10 kilometres of the city, five within 20 kilometres, two within 30 kilometres and two over 40 kilometres away. It should be remembered that three of the projects in the latter two categories are 'new towns'. In eight projects the major employment provision is shared between the project district and the city. In four projects participants are completely dependent on job options within the city, whilst in two cases employment is located, theoretically, entirely within the project location itself.

4.3 Site Planning and Infrastructural Development

The amount of land used for residential purposes in the reviewed projects ranges from 19.2 per cent to 65.4 per cent of the total site area (see Table 6). Four projects use less than 35 per cent and only two projects manage to utilize over 60 per cent of the land for housing plots. In some cases rather low gross densities of housing plots per hectare result partly from the marshy nature of the site land which necessitates the utilization of quite large tracts for dyke and bund flood protection, pumping stations, and so on. This is the case in the Rangsit project in Bangkok and the Bekasi Perumnas project in Jakarta. However, generally speaking, high standards regarding roads and access are the major causes. In nine projects over 20 per cent of the land is utilized for these purposes. The right of way widths of major roads range from 12 to 36 metres. Whilst main pedestrian walkways vary between 2 and 9 metres (see Table 7). One example of excessive standards of circulation provision is the Metroville I project in Karachi with main roads of 36 metres wide and a total of 28.9 per cent of the site being allocated for these purposes. In a Thai project, Rangsit phase I, some 5.77 per cent of the total area was originally set aside for car parking. However, subsequent recognition of its inappropriateness has led the National Housing Authority of Thailand to build more dwellings on this area under phase II of the project.

Another factor which contributes to low gross housing densities in the Vashi project, in Bang Plee Bang Bor new town, and at Dagat-Dagatan is the

Table 6 Land use in reviewed projects

Project	Total area of project site (ha)	Residential (% of total area)	Circulation (% of total area)	Facilities (% of total area)	Industrial and commercial (% of total area)	Other uses (% of total area)
Vashi, New Bombay[a]	603.00	19.20	17.60	21.30	34.60	7.10
Rangsit, Bangkok	25.74	44.36	23.80	4.50	0.70	26.60
Tung Song Hong, Bangkok	42.89	60.70	23.30	8.90	4.70	2.30
Bang Plee Bang Bor, Bangkok (phase I)	266.30	23.60	11.96	8.33	39.76	16.35
Dakshinpuri resettlement, Delhi	78.60	32.60	24.85	36.48	5.92	0.17
Arumbakkam, Madras	32.30	45.96	24.80	6.50	14.90	7.76
Baishnavghata-Patuli, Calcutta	118.00	31.35	25.40	14.40	5.08	23.70
Dagat-Dagatan, Manila	377.50	56.68	10.33	10.92	20.00	2.00
Dasmariñas Bagong Bayan, Manila	452.40	56.81	16.65	13.51	13.04	—
Bekasi Perumnas project, Jakarta	101.80	50.09	16.50	6.38	2.45	24.55
Perumnas project, Medan	178.95	58.40	28.90	9.58	—	3.10
Simomulyo resettlement, Surabaya	27.00	65.40	21.20	7.00	2.40	4.01
Metroville I, Karachi	80.00	47.50	33.18	16.80	2.62	—
Gujaini sites and services, Kanpur	74.30	49.10	24.61	12.06	4.16	10.07

[a] Data relate to Vashi township as a whole, of which the sites and services area comprises only 2 hectares.

Table 7 Circulation standards in reviewed projects

Project	Major road (width in m)	Secondary road (width in m)	Tertiary road (width in m)	Main walkway (width in m)	Minor walkway (width in m)
Vashi, New Bombay	22	11-14	11.0	2.0	1.0
Rangsit, Bangkok	12	—	—	6.5	—
Tung Song Hong, Bangkok	12	8	6.0	4+	3.0-4.0
Bang Plee Bang Bor, Bangkok	32	10	6.0	4.0	—
Dakshinpuri resettlement, Delhi	24	18	13.5	9.0	5.0
Arumbakkam, Madras	15	17	9.0-15.0	4.0	2.0
Baishnavghata-Patuli, Calcutta	30	15	8.0	5.0	3.5
Dagat-Dagatan, Manila	30	20	13.0	9.0	6.0
Dasmariñas Bagong Bayan, Manila	22	9	6.0	4.8	3.0
Bekasi Perumnas project, Jakarta	22	18	13.5	9.0	4.5
Perumnas project, Medan	14	14	7.5	6.0	4.0
Simomulyo resettlement, Surabaya	24	8	6.0	4.0	3.0-4.0
Metroville I, Karachi	36	—	—	3.5	—
Gujaini sites and services, Kanpur	18	14	11.0	2.0	1.0

NB Widths apply to right of way.

Table 8 Water supply standards in reviewed projects

Project	Water consumption supply, litre/person/day	Frequency of supply, hours/day	Number of families per outlet	Fire hydrant, no./hectare	Source of water supply
Vashi, New Bombay	180	24	1.0	4.00	City mains off site
Rangsit, Bangkok	150	15	1.0	0.20	Deep wells on site
Tung Song Hong, Bangkok	200	10	1.0	0.67	Deep wells on site
Bang Plee Bang Bor, Bangkok	250	10	1.0	0.80	Deep wells on site
Dakshinpuri resettlement, Delhi	45	6	1.5	0.50	Tube-wells on site
Arumbakkam, Madras	135	2	1.0	0.37	City mains off site
Baishnavghata-Patuli, Calcutta	100	16	1.0	0.32	Tube-wells on site
Dagat-Dagatan, Manila	105	24	1.0	1.60	Deep wells on site
Dasmariñas Bagong Bayan, Manila	135	12	30–40	0.25	Deep wells on site
Bekasi Perumnas project, Jakarta	80	3	1.0	1.00	Shallow wells on site
Perumnas project, Medan	80	24	1.0	1.00	City mains off site
Simomulyo resettlement, Surabaya	80	24	1.0	1.00	City mains off site
Metroville I, Karachi	135	8	1.0	1.15	City mains connection but no supply as yet off site
Gujaini sites and services, Kanpur	150	16	4.0	0.27	Tube-wells on site

allocation of land for industrial and commercial uses. In Vashi some 34.4 per cent is to be used for these purposes, at Bang Plee 39.7 per cent, at Dagat-Dagatan 20 per cent.

More than half of the projects utilize the existing city networks of water supply and sewerage systems. In six projects these are provided specifically for the project site itself at considerable cost. Provision of water supply varies from 45 litres per person per day to 250 litres per person per day. Some projects have round the clock water supply whilst others are limited to a supply period as low as 2 hours per day (see Table 8). The most common sources of water supply are deep wells and city piped water supply systems. Eleven of the fourteen projects provide individual water connections.

Sewerage systems are a major cost component in all projects, particularly in projects that use water-borne systems where sewage treatment plants are also included in the project plan. Eight projects utilize systems which are not water-borne while six provide water-borne systems (see Table 9). Twelve projects provide individual toilets for each plot and in the two remaining projects, Dakshinpuri and Kanpur, communal toilets are provided.

Table 9 Sewerage and drainage in reviewed projects

Project	Sewerage System	User access	Drainage system
Vashi, New Bombay	Water-borne	Individual household	Open
Rangsit, Bangkok	Septic tanks	Individual household	Closed
Tung Song Hong, Bangkok	Septic tanks	Individual household	Open
Bang Plee Bang Bor, Bangkok	Septic tanks	Individual household	Open
Dakshinpuri resettlement, Delhi	Septic tanks	Communal	Open
Arumbakkam, Madras	Water-borne	Individual household	Closed
Baishnavghata-Patuli, Calcutta	Water-borne	Individual household	Open
Dagat-Dagatan, Manila	Water-borne	Individual household	Open 60% Closed 40%
Dasmariñas Bagong Bayan, Manila	Septic tanks	Individual household	Open. Closed for industrial zone
Bekasi Perumnas project, Jakarta	Septic tanks	Individual household	Open
Perumnas project, Medan	Septic tanks	Individual household	Open
Simomulyo resettlement, Surabaya	Septic tanks	Individual household	Open
Metroville I, Karachi	Water-borne	Individual household	Closed
Gujaini sites and services, Kanpur	Water-borne	Communal	Open

Projects demonstrate more economical tendencies in the provision of drainage. Eleven projects use open drainage systems and only three provide underground conduct systems for stormwater drainage (see Table 9). In the Dasmariñas project only drains in the industrial estate are closed.

In all projects, electricity supply and the provision of individual connections is left to the electricity authority responsible for the locality. In some projects, residents are required to wait until they can afford to pay connection fees and service charges, but all projects envisage eventual private electricity connections for all residents.

A wide range of infrastructural standards have been adopted in the projects themselves but they are predominantly on the high side and reflect a reluctance on the part of implementing authorities to undertake any radical cost cutting experiments along this dimension. The actual standards applied and utilized vary remarkably from project to project. Sometimes this depends on the conditions at the site itself but more often on the prevailing standards in the city regulations. Nevertheless, in practice there is some degree of modification or relaxation of standards in one or more components of all the projects. In the Arumbakkam project in Madras, for example, the standards and specifications followed are lower than those prescribed by the Madras Corporation, the Tamil Nadu Housing Board, and other relevant authorities, but the Madras Metropolitan Development Authority, the authority responsible for designing and coordinating the implementation and maintenance of this scheme, was able to prevail upon the cooperating authorities to relax certain regulations, so that standards could be adopted that meet the needs and affordability of the target groups. Such waiving of regulations in specific areas is often granted to public agencies that undertake such schemes.

The plot size options provided by projects vary widely. Only three projects restrict all their plot options to less than 40 m². In the Baishnavghata-Patuli project in Calcutta, plot options range from 32 to 198 m², and in Metroville I in Karachi plots range from 66 to 333 m² (see Table 10).

The cost problems implicit in high housing standards in sites and services projects are reflected in the cost of on-plot development. Five projects provide no open plot option to prospective project customers and all projects offer at least one core house option but usually they offer three or more (see Table 10). Only seven of these core options from the overall range offered by the reviewed projects cost less than US$500 per unit.* In the cost range between US$500 and 1,000, 14 options overall are available from the reviewed projects.

4.4 Management of Site Development and Construction

Generally, land development work is carried out by several contractors engaged by tender. Only the projects in Thailand restrict land development work to a single contractor. Work on infrastructure and on plot/core house construction is generally given to a single contractor, but sometimes, because of the large scale of a project, this contract is subsequently split up between several contractors. This is the case in seven projects (see Table 11). The

---

* Costs calculated at January 1981 prices.

Table 10 Plot and dwelling options in reviewed projects

Project	Plot option	Plot size (m^2)	Built core area (m^2)	No. of plots	Distribution (%)	Building cost (per unit) (US$)
Vashi, New Bombay	A	36.00	3.34	29	10.00	237.00
	B	36.00	3.34	30	10.50	360.00
	C	36.00	15.00	118	41.25	544.00
	D	36.00	25.00	109	38.25	714.00
			TOTAL	286		
Rangsit, Bangkok	One only	80.00	32.25	1,428	100.00	1,528.25
			TOTAL	1,428		
Tung Song Hong, Bangkok	A1	80.00	20.50	1,565	52.10	1,659.00
	A2.1	80.00	37.80	612	20.40	2,176.90
	A2.2	80.00	37.80	303	10.10	2,255.10
	Core B	80.00	55.10	161	5.40	4,918.40
	Core C1	80.00	55.10	241	8.00	3,062.80
	Core C	80.00	23.04	55	1.80	1,326.20
	Open plot	100.00	—	66	2.20	—
			TOTAL	3,003		
Bang Plee Bang Bor, Bangkok	A	84.00	25.00	1,260	24.20	1,340.00
	B	84.00	38.00	1,902	36.50	1,650.00
	C	160.00	48.00	832	6.00	2,075.00
	D	200.00	84.00	768	14.80	2,960.00
	E	440.00	—	110	2.10	0
	Shophouse 3 storeys	84.00	148.00	133	2.60	9,121.00
	Shophouse 3 storeys	84.00	200.00	200	3.80	12,244.00
			TOTAL	5,205		
Dakshinpuri resettlement Delhi	(EWS) core	20.91	16.77	553	4.20	626.00
	Open plot	20.91	—	12,608	95.80	—
			TOTAL	13,161		
Arumbakkam, Madras	(EWS) 1	40.00	3.50	1,058	45.90	96.00
	(EWS) 2	46.50	18.50	462	20.10	289.80
	(EWS) 3	46.50	28.50	179	7.80	766.00
	(LIG) 4	74.30	—	319	13.80	—
	(MIG) 5	139.40	—	184	8.00	—
	(HIG) 6	223.00	—	102	4.40	—
			TOTAL	2,304		
Baishnavghata-Patuli, Calcutta	(EWS) 1	32.00	—	330	7.00	408.00
	(EWS) 2	32.90	8.06	550	12.00	584.00
	(EWS) 3	40.50	8.90	·1,700	38.00	660.00
	(LIG) 4	54.00	15.20	1,200	27.00	898.00
	(MIG) 5	101.00	—	375	9.00	—
	(MIG) 6	135.00	—	150	4.00	—
	(HIG) 7	198.00	—	130	3.00	—
			TOTAL	4,435		

Project	Plot option	Plot size (m^2)	Built core area (m^2)	No. of plots	Distribution (%)	Building cost (per unit) (US$)
Dagat Dagatan, Manila	A	84–150	—	1,041	28.6	—
	B_3	60–84	n.a. (sanitary core & floor slab)	1,087	30.0	335.50
	B_1	50–72	n.a. (sanitary auxilliary walls, floor slab, & roof)	685	18.8	525.60
	D_3	50–72	n.a. (sanitary core & house core)	805	22.1	1,026.80
	F	60–72	32	19	0.5	3,947.50
	CURRENT PHASE TOTAL			3,637		
Dasmarinas Bagong Bayan, Manila	1	200.00	—	832	13.1	—
	2	100.00	n.a. (sanitary core)	1,900	29.9	n.a.
	3	100.00	30	3,379	53.2	n.a.
	4	100.00	30	226	3.6	n.a.
	5	100.00	36	12	0.2	n.a.
			TOTAL	6,349		
Bekasi Perumnas Project, Jakarta	T24	90.00	24	3,000	65.0	585.20
	T33	90.00	33	500	21.0	1,442.60
	T36	120.00	36	312	14.0	1,473.60
			TOTAL	3,812		
Perumnas project, Medan	Sub-core	90.00	—	629	6.8	—
	Sub-core	60.00	15	403	4.4	556.00
	D21/24	90.00	21/24	4,756	52.0	1,176.00
	D33	90.00	33	2,364	25.8	2,112.00
	D36	90.00	36	1,008	11.0	2,304.00
			TOTAL	9,160		
Simomulyo resettlement, Surabaya	D20	96.00	20	1,276	75.0	600.00
	D36	96.00	36	160	9.5	1,400.00
	D45	96.00	45	160	9.5	1,800.00
	M70	120.00	70	96	6.0	3,500.00
			TOTAL	1,692		
Metroville I, Karachi	1 Open plot	66.00	—	125	3.2	—
	2 Utility wall	66.00	—	2,500	61.0	n.a.
	3 Open plot	100.00	—	75	1.8	—
	4 Utility wall	100.00	—	850	20.7	n.a.
	5 Town house	100.00	n.a.	285	6.9	n.a.
	6 Open plot	200.00	—	185	4.6	—
	7 Open plot	333.00	—	75	1.8	—
			TOTAL	4,095		
Gujaini sites and services, Kanpur	(EWS) I	36.75	1.41	458	11.8	130.50
	(EWS) II	36.75	1.41	538	13.8	436.10
	(EWS) III	36.75	21.28	1,344	34.5	814.00
	(EWS) IV	36.75	21.28	1,548	39.9	962.15
			TOTAL	3,888		

Table 11 Types of contracts tendered in reviewed projects

	Land improvement and infrastructural work contract(s) used	*On-plot core house— construction contracts used*
Vashi, New Bombay	Multi contract	Single contract
Rangsit, Bangkok	Single contract	Single contract
Tung Song Hong, Bangkok	Single contract	Single contract
Bang Plee Bang Bor, Bangkok	Single contract	Single contract (split)
Dakshinpuri resettlement, Delhi	Multi contract	Self-help
Arumbakkam, Madras	Multi contract	Single contract
Baishnavghata-Patuli, Calcutta	Multi contract	Single contract (split)
Dagat-Dagatan, Manila	Multi contract	Single contract
Dasmariñas Bagong Bayan, Manila	Multi contract	Multi contract
Bekasi Perumnas project, Jakarta	Multi contract	Single contract (split)
Perumnas project, Medan	Multi contract	Single contract (split)
Simomulyo resettlement, Surabaya	Multi contract	Single contract (split)
Metroville I, Karachi	Multi contract	Single contract (split)
Gujaini sites and services, Kanpur	Multi contract	Single contract (split)

tendering of contracts is nearly always carried out by the development authority or national housing authority, but usually the day to day decision making and the authority to instruct and pay the contractor(s) are vested in the project manager. However, in some countries, notably Thailand and Indonesia, the system is centralized and the authority to instruct the contractor(s) and release funds for payment rests solely with the main office of the implementing authority.

In most countries the labour required for the work is estimated and specified in the tender in order to achieve the rapid completion of the work involved, and this is made one of the contractual conditions. None of the projects employs the intended residents in infrastructural or core house construction work. Further, to avoid delays in construction, the majority of implementing agencies provide the contractor(s) with essential materials such as cement and steel. In some cases this has led to mismanagement. However, in most of the projects, there are built-in checks in the system to avoid mismanagement. Some of these checks are procedurally complex and time consuming in themselves and therefore prone to delay. In some cases mismanagement has taken place because of the authority's concern to expedite the project.

The majority of the schemes were completed in about 2 to 3 years, but the projects in the Philippines involve larger time frames, from 5 to 10 years because of the size of the schemes, their phased implementation and, in the case of Dagat-Dagatan, because of the large-scale land reclamation work involved.

4.5 Plot Allocation and Tenure Conditions

Usually the allocation of plots is handled after site development by the implementing authorities. In some cases accepted project participants are allotted plots on a first come first served basis, but more often plots are assigned at the discretion of the project agency or by some form of lottery. The three Indonesian projects and the two Philippines projects selected families on the basis of their specific eligibility for each respective project, and the implementing agency (namely Perumnas for the Indonesian projects and the National Housing Authority of the Philippines) retained the prerogative of allotting a particular plot to a particular family. In the Arumbakkam project in Madras, qualifying families from each specific category (see case study VII, chapter 5, for details) participated in a lottery to ascertain which family would occupy which plot. This was also the case in Rangsit and Metroville I projects. In the Baishnavghata-Patuli project in Calcutta and the Tung Song Hong project in Bangkok, where allocation has only been partially carried out, lotteries have been used. Interestingly, in the latter case allocation was done before construction work on site had been completed, but subsequently allotments had to be cancelled and the downpayments returned because of litigation between the NHA of Thailand and the contractor. The NHA took this step because it was clear that prices would change after the legal conflict had been sorted out. Plots in the Gujaini project in Kanpur and the Bang Plee Bang Bor project in Bangkok have not yet been allocated. However, in the case of the latter, it is planned to allot plots one year before they become available to give incoming families time to raise sufficient funds to make their downpayments before actually taking them up.

Six projects allocate plots on a leasehold basis only, with lease periods ranging from 20 to 99 years. The remaining eight projects allow families to purchase the house and land, usually on hire-purchase or a mortgage loan basis, though outright cash purchase is also possible. In one Thai project, the Rangsit project, people could buy the house but would have only long-term leasehold of the land itself.

In most projects there are stipulations concerning the amount of time which may elapse before the plot is occupied by the family to whom it has been allotted. However, enforcement of such regulations appears to have been rather variable. Firm action has been taken on this issue in only a few projects, partly because of mitigating circumstances and reasons brought forward by offending families, such as the need to find new employment closer to the project before moving to the site or the desire to complete their new house before moving. The National Housing Authority of Thailand plans to enforce its rule that allottees occupy their plots within 6 months of the plots becoming available in its current Tung Song Hong and Bang Plee Bang Bor projects. Its experience with its first project, the Rangsit project, in which it did not enforce any rules on the occupancy of a plot by a family to which it had been allotted, has been a negative one and there was clear evidence of rampant clandestine resale. On the other hand, in the Dasmariñas project in the Philippines there were, at the time of the seminar (January 1981), some 169 cases of abandonment of plots. Families claimed that they abandoned their plots either to return to their home provinces or because the site was too remote from their place of work. In its turn, the NHA of the Philippines has adopted a policy of cancelling allocations to families who have given up their plots, either by abandonment or sale, and has instituted a ruling that they can no longer avail themselves of government assistance if they are found squatting again. It is not clear how the NHA can realistically succeed in this punitive measure.

Another problem at Dasmariñas was that of illegal occupancy. In January 1981 there were 242 cases in which families had occupied vacant units without prior clearance and approval from the NHA of the Philippines. By 1 November 1981, the number had risen to 435. Initially the NHA had taken a serious view of illegal occupancy and had contemplated a policy of forcibly ejecting such families from the site. However, there has been a revision of policy and currently the NHA is regularizing tenure of illegal occupants for a 25 per cent premium over the lease/ownership price to avoid subsidizing illegal occupants, whose affordability is judged to be higher than that of the legally allotted occupant families.

In projects where plots are offered on a leasehold basis, no resale is generally allowed according to regulation. However, some project administrations reported difficulty in policing such regulations. In hire purchase ownership situations, resale is generally forbidden until completion of purchase. In cases where outright cash purchase has taken place, resale of the house and plot is usually allowed, although some projects include limiting clauses in the sale contract. In the Vashi project resale is allowed but householders must pay to the City Industrial Development Corporation 50 per cent of the appreciated value of the house and land gained in the resale. In the two (as yet unoccupied) projects in Thailand, the Tung Song Hong project and Bang Plee Bang Bor new town, resale is allowed but for the first 5 years householders can only sell to the NHA. The National Housing Authority of the Philippines allows resale after it has approved the sale arrangement.

Letting part of the house is generally allowed, and in the Vashi project actually encouraged. In most projects this is seen as a legitimate source of supplementary income for the project residents. In certain projects like the Dakshinpuri project in Delhi, renting/letting takes place on a large scale with around 40 per cent of the households engaging in such activities. Project officials generally agree that the letting of rooms is a valid and even vital source of construction finance.

4.6 Construction Assistance and House Development Regulations

Six projects offer or plan to offer construction loans of either cash or building materials to enable occupying families to expedite the development of their plot or core house. In some of the Indian projects it is noted that many families have problems in procuring scarce building materials like cement and steel. Furthermore, because individual families buy supplies in small quantities, they are paying the highest prices. For this reason a system should be considered of supplying loans in the form of building materials which could be purchased in bulk and passed on to the householders, thus allowing the latter to build more economically. However, cash loans for construction purposes do not involve the substantial administrative costs attached to managing actual materials loans which could erode any cost savings achieved in bulk purchase and which could involve the estate management in a dispute. In the Dasmariñas project, a private agency called Freedom to Build Incorporated operates a building supply store that provides a variety of materials at prices considerably below Manila's commercial prices, by circumventing ordinary market channels and by dealing partly in reject and second-hand materials. All its employees are Dasmariñas residents, and among them are several trained carpenters who supply free technical advice and assistance to project residents.

In six projects some form of technical assistance is planned or provided for residents undertaking development of their core houses. The degree to which the residents are directly assisted or supervised varies considerably. In the Tung Song Hong and Bang Plee Bang Bor projects in Thailand, the NHA plans to have several building technicians stationed on site for such purposes. In the Dasmariñas and Dagat-Dagatan projects, assistance is restricted to scrutiny and approval of the families' building plans by site engineers and architects.

In some other projects, like the Rangsit project and the Dakshinpuri resettlement project, the only form of building guidance offered is design alternatives for core house extension. This is made available in the form of prototype dwellings or through brochures containing plans and some information on how to proceed.

Related to such technical assistance are project regulations on standards of construction and building materials as well as restrictions on where structures could be erected on the plots. On the latter issue, all projects have, or plan to have, some stipulations, although some allow far greater freedom than others. So, too, on the matter of materials. Several projects allow the use of low-quality and second-hand materials with only minimal regulations concerning fire and safety hazards. Other projects' regulations insist on standard materials for any house construction or extension. In the Arumbakkam project in Madras, the incoming families are allowed to use very temporary low-standard materials in the first 6 months, but are required to use materials of durable quality for permanent construction. The Dagat-Dagatan project imposes a similar time limit on temporary construction. In projects where core house development and, particularly, house extension require the formal submission of building plans to various municipal or metropolitan authorities, a considerable degree of inconvenience and delay results for the applying family. In one project, the Arumbakkam project in Madras, some useful steps have been taken to overcome this difficulty. To save the residents time, energy, and patience in approaching the Madras Corporation, the Madras Metropolitan Development Authority, and the Tamil Nadu Housing Board separately weekly meetings of appropriate officials from the three authorities have been arranged at the site. At these meetings residents' plans are scrutinized and corrected where necessary, and building permits are issued there and then.

In none of the reviewed projects are incoming families organized into groups for mutual aid in the development of plots or the construction of core house units. Nevertheless, in several projects groups of families spontaneously carry out house development work together. In the Rangsit project and at Dasmariñas, for example, about 10 per cent of project families carry out part of their house construction and house extension activities in small groups. These groups usually consist of several project families, together with assorted relatives and friends. At Dasmariñas, the mutual-aid construction is stimulated to a considerable degree by the small savings clubs called 'paluwagan' which groups of families organize among themselves. In the Simomulyo project in Surabaya, most of the house extension activity was done by spontaneously formed groups of neighbours who would rotate their efforts between the households until all had completed the extensions they wanted. Individual self help house construction takes place on a much larger scale, although the majority of the householders usually engage skilled builders and artisans to carry out the bulk of permanent house development activities. However, they and their relatives and friends may supply the unskilled labour necessary for such activities. Nevertheless, in many projects self help construction often results in very good-quality housing development.

4.7 Estate Management, Maintenance, and Community Development

The range of functions of and the degree of authority vested in the estate management of the reviewed projects varies considerably from project to project.

In some projects the activities include recruitment, allocation, relocation services (to bring incomng residents from their former abode to the project site), temporary housing provision (while families complete the first stages of housing construction), and orientation of the accepted families to project goals. In the Dasmariñas project, for example, transportation is provided for families in cases where they are being relocated from squatter settlements that are being upgraded or demolished. In the later phases of Dagat-Dagatan project, efforts have been made to arrange community meetings and to disseminate information about the project among the recruited families prior to relocation.

More generally, however, estate management is mainly concerned with providing technical and physical services to project residents as well as social services and economic support services. In addition, estate management is nearly always responsible for maintaining community control; for policing repayments, rules, regulations, and the like; and, at least in the initial years, for maintenance (either directly, or coordinating the work of other agencies).

Most projects experience difficulties in the collection of payments, especially in regard to families who default for long periods of time. Although most have specific policies and procedures for serving notices of eviction after a specified period of default, various circumstances, often relating to real economic hardship, make estate managements reluctant to be overzealous in this regard. This experience indicates that more appropriate policies need to be developed, and collection procedures in some cases need to be tightened up. The National Housing Authority of Thailand, for example, which had fared very poorly in payment collection in the Rangsit project, has developed more stringent procedures for its later projects, Tung Song Hong and Bang Plee Bang Bor.

The provision of social and economic support services is often carried out in conjunction with other government and non-government (voluntary) agencies. In the Dakshinpuri project in New Delhi and the Arumbakkam project in Madras, day-care centres and some income generation programmes are handled by charitable and religious organizations. In the two Philippine projects training to develop people's skills and assistance in entrepreneurial activities by community members are provided by the government agencies concerned.

Carrying out maintenance in the initial years of the project, and the handing over of such maintenance to the appropriate authorities (and, for particular elements, to the people themselves), causes estate management considerable difficulties. In the former case it is sometimes difficult for the implementing agencies to enlist the cooperation of the respective utility authority. In both the Vashi project and the Arumbakkam project, difficulties arose in the handling over of infrastructural elements like roads, water supply, and sewerage to the relevant agencies, due to the adoption of standards and specifications in the project that did not conform to the existing standards of the agencies concerned. At Arumbakkam, it took considerable negotiation to persuade the Madras Metropolitan Water Supply and Sewerage Board to take over maintenance of on-site sewerage lines and water supply lines, because they ran through private properties (i.e. household plots). The delay in handing over sewer and water lines caused further expenditure on maintenance by the Tamil Nadu Housing Board, and added to project cost.

In six of the projects reviewed, specific maintenance charges are either planned or operational. In some projects, for example the Vashi project and the Dasmiriñas project, it is planned to administer such a maintenance charge through a residents' association. The association would collect maintenance fees and organize the community to carry out elements of maintenance—for example, maintenance of community facilities like meeting halls, day-care centres, and so on.

On the community development side, the project experiences are not very positive. The estate management often encounters problems, partly because of the novelty of this kind of project and the kind of management and managerial staff that are required, and partly because of the conflicting roles imposed upon project management by virtue of their extensive range of activities. On the one hand, they are the project policemen, so to speak, enforcing rules and evicting delinquent residents, and on the other, they are the project social workers extending patience, goodwill and understanding to families who have difficulties in their new neighbourhood. Common project experience is that the relocation process, in itself, causes considerable upheaval for some families, and that the scale of the project often works against the estate management's capacity to give special assistance to families experiencing serious difficulties, both economic and social. It is the estate management that has to bear the brunt of such problems, a fact which project designers are often unable to perceive.

4.8 Case Study Focus

The case studies in this chapter are the Vashi project, New Bombay, and the Simomulyo resettlement project, Surabaya. The target population for Vashi did not come from a particular slum but was recruited from various slum and squatter areas in Bombay. The Simomulyo project, however, undertook the resettlement of a particular squatter settlement which was frequently exposed to flood hazards. The Simomulyo resettlement project was able to avoid many of the problems encountered at Vashi because it was addressed to an identified group of slum dwellers. However, the Vashi project demonstrates greater economy in terms of land use, unit cost, and infrastructural investment.

Case Study V VASHI, NEW BOMBAY

(I) Urban Context

At the turn of the century the population of Greater Bombay was a mere 1 million. By 1951 the city had a population of around 3 million and by 1976 it had reached 7.45 million.

The city's development began with the Fort located at the southernmost tip of the island, and since that time this district had remained the central business area of the city. The eastern side of the island provides an excellent deep-water port. The development of the port and the related trading facilities further stimulated the growth of industries on the island. Thus, by the 1970s more than 50 per cent of the city's population lived on the island at a gross population density of more than 445 persons per hectare.

In recent years the trend towards population concentration in the south has been aggravated by land reclamation projects near the island's southern tip for office block construction. City development policies during the same period have tended to permit more intensive development in the island's southern area.

Many middle and lower income residents, particularly those younger families in search of accommodation, are forced to seek homes further north while their jobs remain in the south. For those already domiciled in the southern part of the city, the increasing demand for accommodation there has caused extreme congestion and a deterioration of civic amenities and living conditions generally.

The very shape of Bombay — it is wedge-shaped with most of the activity located at the point of the wedge — allows no possibility of lateral growth. Therefore, to diffuse job activities from southern Bombay, a distribution centre in the north is proposed, together with the development of a city to the east, across the harbour. This new city, New Bombay, is intended to siphon off population and jobs from the Greater Bombay region and also to absorb new urban migrants from the hinterland.

New Bombay is planned to comprise a series of smaller townships (nodes), each of about 100,000 people, ranged along the proposed Mass Rapid Transit Line and collectively forming a city of around 2 million. Vashi is the first such node to be planned and it is currently being developed to accommodate 150,000 people.

(II) Agencies in Project Design and Implementation

The City and Industrial Development Corporation (CIDCO) is responsible for the design and implementation of the whole New Bombay development. The central government finance agency, the Housing and Urban Development Corporation (HUDCO) makes loans available to enable the project residents to pay for their houses and house development.

Decisions in project formulation and implementation are made by various departments of CIDCO. Planning is carried out by the Planning, Social Services, and Economics sections in collaboration with the Engineering section. Financial monitoring and control are managed by the Accounts and Finance section, but the Economics sections prepares the cost and feasibility report. Actual implementation is managed by the Engineering section which calls for tenders from private contractors. The marketing of houses and plots is carried out by the Marketing section. The Estate Management section is responsible for the collection of amortization payments and maintenance dues and for liaison with the community residents. The Social Services section develops various social organizations and people's groups to carry out other activities of use and benefit to the community.

The decision to undertake a sites and services project at Vashi was taken in 1973 and the design and layout of the project took place in that year. HUDCO approved the project in December 1974. Infrastructural work and core house construction took place between December 1974 and March 1976. Applications from prospective residents were called for in January 1976. Allotment and occupation of the units was completed by May 1976.

(III) Target Groups for Vashi Township

It was anticipated that around 60 per cent of Vashi's population would be in the Economically Weaker Section (EWS) and Low Income Group (LIG).

Most of these people would be working in the informal economic sector, the service sector, or lowly paid levels of the formal sector. Thus the target population for the scheme was not drawn from a particular slum but came from various slums and poor housing areas of Bombay and around the project area (New Bombay). In general, most of the incoming households were barely at survival level or were below survival level economically. Given their poor economic circumstances it is (as far as possible) appropriate for them to live near their work places. The sites and services scheme at Vashi, which forms an integral part of the Vashi node, was the first attempt to absorb some families from the EWS category.

To provide housing opportunities for these families is a difficult task because of the high cost of developed land and construction, and because of their extremely limited ability to pay. In order to make land available to them within their paying capacity it was decided to cross subsidize the land cost by selling some plots in the private housing market at a profit so that the remaining plots sold at below market rates would be within the reach of people of modest means.

(IV) Land Acquisition and Improvement

The land selected for this housing scheme site was vacant marshy land. It was chosen because it was easy to acquire, because it was proximate to the State Expressway (which forms the southern tip of Vashi township) and to Greater Bombay itself, and because it was close to the established industries on the Trans Tana Belt. The sites and services project land was located near the already complete sector 1 of Vashi township which had been provided with all the necessary physical infrastructure and social utilities and amenities. Sector 1 also contained a fairly good mix of various income groups which would be proximate and therefore economically useful in terms of employment opportunities to the incoming, very low income sites and services project residents.

The sites and services land was acquired under the Land Acquisition Act of 1894 by the state government and subsequently handed over to CIDCO. Following this, the project land was reclaimed by constructing a dyke and bund. This made the land available quickly and minimized the cost of reclamation.

(V) Site Planning and Infrastructural Development

This sites and services scheme, on a site of 1.92 hectares, is an integral part of the residential area of Vashi township for which the overall percentage of land (excluding the land earmarked for the Agricultural Produce Market which will serve the Bombay region) under residential use is 19.2 per cent (see Table 6, p.67, and site plan). The actual breakdown of land use within the sites and services sector itself is as follows:

Residential: 10,029 m^2—53 per cent of project land.
Circulation: 621 m^2—5 per cent of project land.
Circulation (pedestrian): 2,232 m^2—11 per cent of project land.
Open spaces and institutional: 6,133 m^2—31 per cent of project land.

Construction of the off-site infrastructure was carried out separately by the town level development programme, whereas on-site infrastructure within the project, such as pathways, stormwater drainage, and sewerage, was carried out on separate contracts by different agencies. Most of the public facilities, such as shops and schools, were already constructed in the adjoining sector.

The project area is accessible via a secondary metre wide peripheral road with some of the internal areas accessible via 11 metre wide roads. Individual houses are accessible by means of a network of pathways of not more than 2 metres in width (see Table 7, p.68). The houses are oriented towards the pedestrian spine which links houses to shopping areas, the transportation network (buses), and other public facilities. Over the past 4 years there has been no demand from the residents for the improvement of internal roads and pathways which suggests that there is no need to upgrade them as yet.

At the Vashi township level, the sites and services area is linked to the other township neighbourhoods and industrial and commercial areas by a network of major roads of 22 metres or more in width. This network ultimately connects to a city expressway. Only 50 per cent of the major and secondary road areas have been costed to the scheme.

The Maharashtra Industrial Development Corporation (MIDC) developed three sources of water supply around New Bombay, namely the Baravi, the Patal Ganga, and the Ransai water supply schemes. The MIDC laid trunk lines from the supply sources to distribution points. CIDCO laid the water supply pipeline from these trunk lines and has provided a network of distributory mains to provide a 24 hour water supply to the township and the sites and services scheme. The water passes through a filtration process to make it potable. The internal system is designed to meet household requirements on the basis of 180 litres per capita per day and meets fire protection needs through a system of roadside fire hydrants that permits tapping at 40 metre intervals. Water consumption metres are either provided individually or to groups of 80 to 100 households. The latter reduces installation and maintenance costs. Water charges in January 1981 were about Rs 35 or 21 cents (US) per cubic metre of water consumed.

The new urban centre in which the project is located is provided with an underground water-borne sewerage system. Individual units are connected to a pipe system which feeds into the main sewers laid on the road network. The trunk sewers are made of concrete and are laid for the sewerage needs of the whole area. The system has been designed with consideration for the standards of water supply. Pumphouses are provided to facilitate disposal of sewage from the area to the treatment plant which carries out primary and secondary treatment to the standards specified by the Indian Standards Institute and the Maharashtra Prevention for Water Pollution Board.

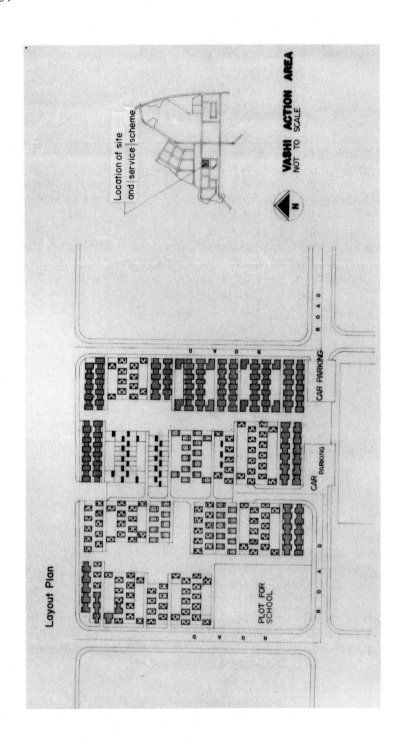

INDEX	TYPE	CARPET AREA	BUILD UP AREA	SALE PRICES	UNIT NOS.	PLOT AREA
■	A	2.55 m²	3.34 m²	Rs 3000.00	29	36 m²
▓	B	2.55 m² / 11.65 m²	3.34 m² / 11.65 m² (PLINTH)	Rs 3500.00	30	36 m²
▦	C	13.00 m²	10.00 m²	52 00.00	118	36 m²
▨	D	23.35 m²	25.00 m²	67 00.00	109	36 m²

TOTAL AREA IN HECTARES: 1.92 (EXCLUDING SCHOOL)   TOTAL POPULATION: 1430

TOTAL OF DWELLINGS / PLOTS: 286   DWELLING DENSITY/HECTARE: 148 NOS.

Site plan: Arumbakkam project, Madras

The drainage system is designed for rainfall to the intensity of 23 centimetres in 3 hours. The system consists of rectangular drains with pipe culverts at road crossings. These drains are in turn connected to the main drainage channel which takes care of precipitation from the whole area and it feeds into a holding pond. The water thus collected is let out to sea through an outlet pipe during low tide. When hide tide coincides with a heavy downpour, the water is pumped out.

Garbage collection boxes are provided for each small cluster of households and subsequently refuse is transported to a refuse disposal dump, which ultimately uses it for land fill. The collection and disposal system is designed to handle approximately 0.2 kilograms of garbage per person per day.

The Maharashtra State Electricity Board (MSEB) is responsible for the generation and distribution of electricity to New Bombay and hence to Vashi. Vashi township is connected by a 110 kV circuit line to Kalwa receiving station, and for internal distribution a network of 22 kV overhead cables has been installed. The entire supply, installation, maintenance, and collection of payment is handled by the MSEB.

(VI) Social Infrastructure and Facilities

The educational needs of the new township are met in the following way. The actual school buildings are constructed by CIDCO on the land set aside for such a purpose. The building is then turned over to state educational institutions which buy the school on easy terms of loan repayment. Private educational institutions can also buy land to construct their own buildings at 5 per cent premium over the base price. Vocational training institutes are constructed and run by CIDCO itself to give vocational training to project members.

Many private medical practitioners have built clinics in other housing areas adjacent to the Vashi sites and services estate. Hospitals are built and handed over to medical and health authorities on the same basis as the educational institutions mentioned above. CIDCO sponsors the community run clinics for the Vashi residents.

Police and fire protection stations are the responsibility of the respective local authorities. An area for each station has been provided. In the case of the fire station, CIDCO has gone ahead and built a structure for this purpose which will be handed over to the authority in due course.

Various sports and religious facilities are being developed by the community in conjunction with non-government organizations. The land areas for social facilities such as schools, hospitals, and recreation have been provided according to the norms prescribed by the state government.

(VII) On-plot Development

The contract for core house/dwelling construction was given to a single contractor who was also responsible for drainage up to the inspection chamber.

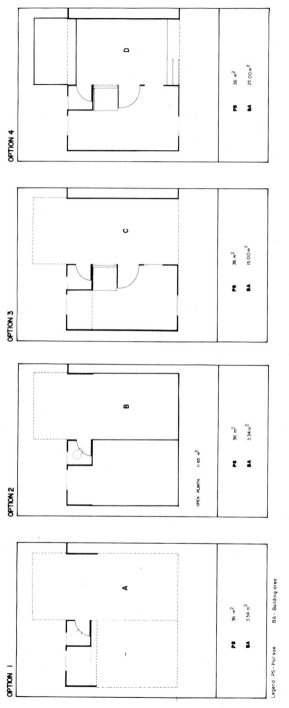

Dwelling options: Bang Plee Bang Bor project, Bangkok

CIDCO supplied some building materials, such as cement, to the building contractor. In the course of core house construction it was noticed that it was difficult to obtain a proper standard of work from the contractor who used the excuse that the poor quality of building materials and design limited his ability to deliver quality.

Only one plot size option, a 36 m^2 plot, was available in the project. There were four dwelling options ranging from type A, a basic sanitary core of 3.34 m^2, to type D, a 25 m^2 fully built house with an open verandah. Each option was fitted with an individual toilet. Types C and D demonstrate the appropriate method of house extension for core house plots in options A and B (see diagrams of dwelling options).

(VIII) Selection and Allocation, Terms of Tenure and Repayment

The main criteria set for the selection of residents for Vashi were that the family own no land and that its monthly income should not exceed US$50 per month. Households had to apply to CIDCO on prescribed forms with an approved certificate of income; then lots were drawn to select people. The actual choice of house was allowed on a first come first served basis.

The house and land are registered under the prevailing Act with the Registrar of Lands. The developed land is made available to the residents on a 60 year lease, with a lease premium to be paid as the land price, either through a loan or as an outright payment, with an annual ground rent of US$0.13 per plot. People who paid outright can sell their lease, but 50 per cent of the appreciation value must be paid back to CIDCO. Those who pay in instalments have to repay the loan completely before sale is permissible. There is no restriction on letting part of the house, and many households finance their housing extension with income earned from renting a room, and it is common for tenants to pay a lump sum of one year's rent in advance.

(IX) Financial Arrangements

CIDCO spends 25 per cent of its budget on housing and draws most of its finance for this purpose from HUDCO. Thus, a crucial factor in sites and services project formulation involves satisfying the norms and standards of HUDCO regarding the construction cost and sale price of dwelling units. Individual loans to the families are financed by HUDCO as well.

Occupants have to pay a minimum of one third of the unit cost as a down payment and the remaining two thirds are covered by the HUDCO loan. The loan is disbursed by CIDCO. It collects residents' repayments on a monthly basis and reimburses HUDCO on a quarterly basis.

Initially CIDCO provided loan facilities to all allottees through HUDCO at 5 per cent interest per annum for 20 years with monthly repayments. The details of initial downpayments and monthly instalments for various options are shown in Table 12.

Table 12 Initial down payments and monthly instalments at Vashi

Type	Initial payment (US$)	Monthly payment (US$)	Number of instalments
A	169.00	2.00	240
A	173.00	2.70	240
C	236.00	4.00	240
D	305.00	5.20	240

Generally the land provided for housing the Economically Weaker Section and the Low Income Group is subsidized, but care is taken to recover all capital costs involved in land development. This is recovered through the sale of commercial plots and residential plots intended for higher income groups elsewhere in the new township at market prices. The land development cost is cross subsidized for all EWS and LIG residents, but not the building costs of the core housing.

The maintenance costs for the common areas are recovered from the individual households by the residents' association. CIDCO has taken the initiative in forming these associations so that maintenance can be the community's responsibility.

(X) Dwelling Improvement and Extension by Project Participants

No construction loans, either in cash or in materials, are extended to the residents by the implementing agency. Nevertheless, nearly all households have taken some steps to develop and finish off their houses. They finance their house improvement by raising personal loans from employers and friends, or from social security savings, personal savings, or income gained through letting rooms. For completion of the core house itself residents do not have to go to the Estate Management section of CIDCO for permission. However, for any extension of the house that involves creating additional built-up area (beyond the area indicated for type D), they must seek such permission and appoint a qualified architect to supervise the work. Most of the work is carried out by skilled masonry contractors but the building materials are supplied by the individuals. In most cases people have used second-hand building materials, especially for doors, windows, and roofing, but the materials are of durable quality. A more difficult issue is the procurement of cement for construction, because it is a controlled commodity.

Developments carried out include all plastering, flooring, and creating an extra room by enclosing the open verandah (when the house has been developed to type D stage). A few have extended their house to fill the entire plot of 36 square metres.

To facilitate the completion of the house and the subsequent extension of the built-up area, the project estate management considers that materials like cement should be supplied to the residents in limited quantities on a priority basis. Another suitable strategy would be to supply them with information regarding cost advantages and methods for sharing various materials purchased collectively in bulk, because the purchasing of such materials in small quantities costs them more.

(XI) Occupancy Changes and Title Transfers

It has been observed that about 75 per cent of the house in the project have been resold. This is so because the initial recipients of the EWS units, having monthly incomes of around US$47 per month, faced prohibitively high housing expenditures of around US$12 per month when property taxes and water and electricity costs were added to monthly repayments. Another factor contributing to changes of occupancy was that many of those who were allotted housing units had their work places in Bombay and thus incurred additional expenses for transportation. The project design left employment generation to the initiative of the individuals and, for EWS families, such opportunities are still mainly available in Bombay itself.

The fact that such a financially attractive housing scheme was not available to the Middle Income Group meant that interested families from this group provided a ready market for EWS families who were having difficulties or who wanted to speculate. Interestingly, many poorer families from the MIG are growing families who have insufficient savings to pay the initial downpayment but have the earning capacity to pay the higher monthly rent.

Case Study VI SIMOMULYO RESETTLEMENT, SURABAYA, INDONESIA

(I) Urban Context

In 1976 the port city of Surabaya had an estimated population of 2.1 million of whom 200,000 people were not permanent residents. At that time the shortfall in housing provision was estimated at 68,000 units. By 1981 this was estimated at well over 130,000 dwelling units.

Overall the quality of the housing stock and infrastructural conditions in the city is fairly low. Less than 20 per cent of the total housing stock is permanent. Many areas of the city suffer from seasonal flooding which sometimes ravages kampongs located along the riverbanks. Households living in these kampongs do so on the basis of complicated land tenure agreements, some legal but mostly illegal. Most houses are owned by the families occupying them.

The municipality of Surabaya has been taking measures to overcome flooding problems in the city, mainly along the River Brenta Hilir and the Kalimas canal. The Simomulyo resettlement project was undertaken in an effort to reduce flooding and the subsequent costs to the city, by resettling families who were legally or illegally living on the banks of the waterways in these frequently flooded areas.

The project involved relocating approximately 2,500 families in the project site about 8 kilometres west of the commercial centre of the city. The municipality has been encouraging development in this area in order to counterbalance the city's natural spread to the south and south-east. However, traditional industries are harbour-related and therefore located in the north of the city, whilst new factories are located mostly in the south. This means that project families would still remain dependent on employment opportunities in the inner city area as job opportunities in the areas surrounding Simomulyo are limited to the construction sector.

(II) Agencies in Project Design and Implementation

After receiving a proposal from the municipal government of Surabaya for the relocation scheme, the central government instructed Perumnas, the National Urban Development Corporation of Indonesia, to design and implement the scheme in cooperation with the local authorities. The municipal government decided upon the policy, the terms of compensation, and the location of the project. However, as it lacked sufficient funds, an agreement was reached with Perumnas whereby the latter funded the entire design and implementation of the scheme. Nevertheless, the local government did contribute indirectly in so far as it paid compensation to resettling families and sold the site land to Perumnas for a price (US$1.00 per square metre) that was well below the market price.

Project design and implementation were carried out by Perumnas which usually functions as a very centralized national agency. However, for a project of this type, where day to day cooperation and inputs from the municipal government of Surabaya and other government agencies such as the Municipal Water Supply Agency (PDAM) and the State Electricity Agency (PLN) were required, it was necessary to deviate from such a centralized approach. There were time constraints, too, which necessitated rapid execution of the project. Therefore, in order rapidly to implement a relocation project of this magnitude, the project manager had to have wide powers of decision making. If the usual centralized decision making procedures had both used, any minor but necessary revisions of the design and management system could not have been made without incurring extended delays.

(III) The Target Group

The people who were resettled at Simomulyo were generally very poor. Average monthly earnings per household amounted to about US$50. About 80 per cent of household heads had regular jobs or entrepreneurial occupations such as running repair shops and stands, carpentry shops and foodstalls. Some 20 per cent were under-employed or unemployed.

As their economic circumstances were quite precarious, care had to be taken in project design to provide appropriate, informal economic opportunities for them. Most importantly, a cheap and frequent transportation service to the city had to be arranged.

(IV) Site Preparation, Housing, and Infrastructural Development

The low-lying land was not filled as this would have been too expensive. Instead, a dyking system was constructed. After the site had been prepared by the local government body, Perumnas carried out the site planning. The site planning in this project maximized construction management efficiency by using standardized land use modules. Rapid road and drainage construction was facilitated by involving actual contractors as early as possible so that realistic contracts could be negotiated and full comprehension of the organization of the work, the scheduling of development phases, and advance ordering of building materials, could be achieved.

Infrastructural work including roads, drainage, and septic tanks for sewage disposal was publicly tendered early in the design stage and carried out in the implementation stage by private contractors. Public utility authorities were responsible for the installation and connection of the water and electricity supplies.

The Simomulyo site of 27 hectares has been developed with a land use distribution (see Table 6 for comparison with other reviewed projects) as follows:

Residential	17.66 hectares	65.4 per cent of total area
Circulation	5.72 hectares	21.2 per cent of total area
Facilities	1.89 hectares	7.0 per cent of total area
Commercial	0.65 hectares	2.4 per cent of total area
Miscellaneous	1.08 hectares	4.0 per cent of total area

The site planning approach employed the standardization of plot sizes and dwelling units in order to maximize the efficiency of construction. Thus, only two plot sizes were designed, of 96 and of 120 square metres (both modules of 12).

Core house and completed house construction were carried out by private contractors. The basic building components were produced in advance by a single manufacturer to achieve a low unit price and uniformity of quality. This enabled structures to be erected rapidly, and helped to guarantee an even profit margin for the contractors involved in the construction of the 1,692 units.

All construction of infrastructure and housing units conformed to standards developed and applied by Perumnas in other projects. These standards are very close to national and Surabaya master plan standards. The site was ready for occupation only 7 months after Perumnas had received the project proposal.

(V) Allocation, Dwelling Options, and Tenure

Each family from the nominated riverside areas, regardless of its legal status of occupancy (owner, tenant, or squatter), was given the option to move to the resettlement area. Free transportation was arranged by the project management to enable householders to transfer their possessions to the new location.

Four dwelling types were made available in this project. The D.20 core house constructed at a unit cost of US$600 (in 1977) accounted for 1,276 of the total number (75 per cent). Its built-up area of 20 m^2 consists of a single room with a sanitary cell inside it. The D.36 and D.45 types are simple shell houses of 36 and 45 m^2 of built-up area respectively, together with an internal sanitary cell. A combined total of 320 units of these two types were constructed at a unit cost of US1,440 for the D.36 and US$1,800 for the D.45. The M.70 with 70 m^2 floor area is a fully built two-storey maisonette costing US$3,500 per unit. Only 96 of these were constructed.

The housing units were initially taken up on a long-term leasehold basis. After two years of residence the lease of the core house can be changed to hire purchase ownership, but the land remains in government ownership. In the case of the D.20 core house, allottees had to make a downpayment of US$20.00 (which included a US$5.00 charge for the water supply connection) with the balance payable in monthly instalments of $10.00 over 20 years. These monthly payments include water, electricity, and maintenance charges.

(VI) Dwelling Completion and Extension

No loans in either cash or building materials were supplied to core house residents. All further house development costs were financed privately. Residents were allowed to use old materials from their former houses to complete the core houses. Although there was a set of guidelines for extending the house by the allottees, it has been largely ignored. The project management realized the need to be flexible in this regard. Extensions vary in extent and quality in accordance with the resources of the individual families. Most family building activity was carried out by the occupants themselves with the help of friends and neighbours. Some technical advice and assistance was provided by the Perumnas project management. As yet no clear rules have been established on how to compensate an occupant for the self-financed development and extension of the core house if he wishes to move out from the project before he has acquired ownership of the core house.

Chapter 5

Financing Sites and Services

5.1 Cost Recovery and Replicability

A significant policy element underlying the sites and services strategy is the emphasis on cost recovery which enables shelter programmes to be developed that can be replicated on a large scale. In essence this means that all costs involved in the project, from the cost of land to that of the administrative and technical expertise, should be borne by the people without any subsidy whatsoever.

The number of people in need of housing is so enormous that any housing solution involving subsidies at all must, for equity reasons, distribute them over a vast number of families. Since the finance that can be directed as subsidies to low income families generally is very limited, the cost of the housing must be almost totally met by the people themselves.

However, the goal of full cost recovery has remained an elusive one. Of the 60 or more sites and services projects carried out with the World Bank's financial support, none has yet achieved full cost recovery. The World Bank's stress on cost recovery is prompted by two other factors besides the arithmetic realities of the resources–needs equation.

The first factor is that 'the existence of government subsidies has meant that very little pressure has been exerted towards the use of appropriate design standards and, by the same token, towards the control of cost' (Churchill, 1980, p.13). In other words, an inbuilt commitment to the economic use of resources can have an impact on the development of more suitable designs and technologies. Secondly, the World Bank considers cost recovery to be essential if private developers are to be encouraged to replicate these low-cost housing solutions on a large scale. On the cost recovery record of sites and services schemes generally, it is not surprising that the private sector has shown no interest as yet.

Of the nine reviewed projects that had already been implemented and at least partially occupied, only three had made real achievements in terms of cost recovery. Some of the other projects had been consciously designed to distribute various levels of subsidy to their participants. The components of real costs most frequently omitted in the pricing of plots were land, administrative overheads, and part of the interest on construction and mortgage loans.

The actual repayment collection performance of the reviewed projects is discussed in Chapter 6.

5.2 Ability and Willingness to Pay

Several conditions are necessary if a serious attempt is to be made to achieve cost recovery. The first is that the house and services must be within the people's ability to pay. To ensure that this is so, it is necessary to identify clearly all project costs and then to determine a formula for their recovery. This in turn requires a clear understanding of what the target households can afford and, further, what they are willing to pay for. Identification of what householders' priorities are enables project designers to cut down on items that are not so important to the people themselves. When people are not forced to pay for components which they themselves do not consider a priority (at that particular point in time) it enhances both their ability and their willingness to pay. Hence, the participation of the potential residents in the design and implementation of projects is an important precondition for cost recovery, especially in so far as services are concerned.

Although such a process of involving the people, or consulting them in choices and decisions, and of seeking their agreement and consent is an arduous and unfamiliar one, it can contribute directly to mobilizing the people's energies, resources, and goodwill. This, in turn, can have a pro- found impact on the implementation of the project and on sustaining the momentum necessary to its success. The evidence to date suggests that the absence of such participation seriously impedes the implementation of a project and undermines the cost recovery mechanism. A related factor that contributes to willingness to pay is security of land tenure. Although this is more important in slum upgrading schemes, it is none the less significant in sites and services projects. In all projects except the Dakshinpuri project in New Delhi, long-term security of tenure has been provided in the form of long- term leasehold or freehold ownership. In all cases payment in instalments was offered as an option. In the Dasmariñas project tenure resulted in settlers being offered the right to purchase their plots outright, if they so desired. The provision of secure tenure supplies a resident with a vested interest in the community environment as a whole, as well as in the gradual development of his own housing. Thus, tenure is vital to cost recovery and the financial viability of the project. It is also the main catalyst to housing investment by sites and services residents.

It is important that householders in a sites and services project be given as much freedom as possible in the use of their housing. The right to let rooms and to use their dwelling for legal, productive activities that can earn income should be extended to the residents. Some project agencies are inclined to look at a low income sites and services project as if it were a middle-class housing estate and, therefore, feel justified in proscribing activities that might detract from the pleasant appearance of the site. Such proscriptive rules, generally emphasizing the separation of functions, are incongruous to the sites and services approach.

In the particular urban context in which sites and services action is being considered, an up-to-date and thorough survey should be made of low income housing conditions and household employment and incomes. Such a survey makes possible clear perceptions of which low income groups could utilize assistance, in the form of improved housing options in the eventual sites and services project, and which groups could not, because their incomes are too low or too high. With the data accumulated, it is then possible to set about selecting a site and acquiring land. If some land has been acquired before this low income housing survey, then the survey should establish whether the sites are suitable for projects. Then the physical design of a project site, the plot sizes and core house options, and infrastructure standards to be used can be calculated realistically from the survey data, which should reveal both the ability and willingness of the target group to pay for what it is going to acquire. Nevertheless, care must be taken when making such estimates because of the extreme vulnerability of low income groups to economic factors as inflation, and because the move to a new location usually increases household expenditure (housing costs and transportation) and may reduce income earning opportunities (either by loss of opportunity or loss of time due to the greater distance from the employment opportunity).

5.3 Calculating Total Project Costs

In view of the above considerations, it is clear that a pricing policy for sites and services plots must involve a comprehensive analysis of the real costs involved in the particular project. The World Bank paper on sites and services provided the following checklist of items (International Bank for Reconstruction and Development, 1974, p.45):

(a) Detailed estimates of total project costs (first costs):
—Land acquisition, compensation
—Site preparation including topo/survey works, earthworks, clearing and levelling, staking out of plot boundaries, road centering, etc.
—Off-site public utilities including project specific trunk infra-structure and plants
—On-site public utilities including water supply, sewerage, surface drainage, roads and footways, public lighting and electricity, telephone
—Community facilities including project specific schools, health clinics, community centres, markets, shops, small industries, fire, police, postal, garbage disposal
—Plot development including all costs associated with development of individual plots in the form of construction costs and/or material loans

— Supervision
— Engineering
— Administration
— Technical assistance
— Project preparation prior to formal implementation
— Allowances for inflation, price escalation
— Allowances for physical contingencies
— Other
(b) Estimates of recurrent costs for operation and maintenance of project

Some of the above items deserve some comment and clarification before we review the projects' pricing policies and cost recovery performance.

It is clear that land is a significant component of what is being delivered to incoming residents, but there are difficulties involved in ascertaining its value. In cases where the land is acquired from private landowners, it is not always possible to ensure that 'market' prices are not inflated by collusive practices. Certainly, it would be inequitable to make the poor bear the financial burden of paying speculative profits to the rich. Then, on the other hand, there is the situation where the land is already in the hands of public authorities. In such cases there is often the tendency to undervalue the 'market' price of the land, or even to overlook it completely and treat it as a government contribution to the project. But this still amounts to a very significant subsidy and highly subsidized programmes cannot be a realistic alternative to slums and squatter settlements.

The issue of the limited long-term availability of urban land should not be obscured by the current (politically popular) emphasis on assisting the poor (this emphasis is also strongly articulated by international funding agencies). There will be more and more poor families for generations to come. Therefore, as the supply of urban land is finite, a long-range view has to be adopted. Even in cities like Karachi and Bangkok, where government agencies hold quite large tracts of urban land, it cannot be automatically provided free of charge or at below market price without incurring possible diseconomies and injustices in the long term. Only in cases where all land, or a very large proportion, is government held (Karachi is a case in point) could below market price disposal be considered. Even in such cases, however, rivalries between landowning government agencies often prevent the emergence of a rational government land disposal policy.*

Some infrastructural items, too, can be problematic in terms of costing. Depending on the location of the project and whether or not it lies in the direction of intended city growth and development, the cost of access roads, trunk mains for water supply, sewerage and electricity to the project site

---

* See Wegelin (1982a), particularly para. 4.2, for a discussion about such disputes (in an upgrading context) in Karachi.

boundary may or may not be costed and charged completely to the project. World Bank guidelines, however, suggest that it is inappropriate and basically unreasonable if sites and services project participants have to pay for such items when they are normally provided by the public sector for higher income groups without direct charges. The reviewed projects generally adopted this approach. The Dagat-Dagatan project does not recover the costs of off-site infrastructural works from the allottees. Instead, these components are funded by various line agencies as grants. Similarly, the National Housing Authority of Thailand does not plan to charge allottees for off-site infrastructure in its Bang Plee Bang Bor project. These costs are funded by the Ministry of Finance and the Telephone Organization of Thailand as direct subsidies to the project (to be recovered through local rates and telephone charges to subscribers). On-site infrastructural works should be directly attributed to project costs and recovered from the residents. However, in nine seminar projects capital subsidies were either planned for, or were already provided in the case of implemented schemes.

5.4 Marketing Sites and Services

The effective matching of target group ability and willingness to pay for plot/core house options is extremely important for the marketing of sites and services. Too often the notion that the sites and services projects are a form of welfare for underprivileged sections of the community pervades project design and implementation. This has the effect of reducing the effort and resourcefulness that project designers and managers actually exert to provide options that are attractive (in terms of design) and affordable to particular percentiles of the target group. (See chapter 3 for discussion of this issue.) The attitude that the poor should be grateful for any kind of housing opportunity they get fails to take into account the fact that they are critical and capable of making rational choices. The kind of response such an attitude engenders is usually a negative one, which seriously reduces the people's willingness to join the project (if they have a choice). It can set a bad tone for future relations between estate management and the community, and can prove to be a formidable hindrance to debt collection. There is a need to see sites and services project participants as clients or customers. After all, ideally they are paying for what they are getting, and their enthusiasm for what they are buying will bear some connection to their repayment performance.

Often projects fail to disseminate clear and pertinent information to their intended target groups. This failure sometimes results from choosing inappropriate media for reaching particular kinds of people. Whilst the mass media are certainly useful in making initial project information available, project experience shows that door to door approaches, and group meetings in settlements from which participants will be drawn, are more reliable ways to contact and recruit poorer clients. If real efforts are made to inform the chosen target group, then recruitment is faster and more satisfactory in the long term.

Pricing policies for plots in sites and services projects should reflect their potential land values. Obviously, there will be differences in this regard between plots in different locations in the project, between different land uses and, to a lesser extent, between plots having different sizes. Too often projects set across-the-board plot prices without considering differential land pricing as a possible option to maximize cost recovery within the affordability of the various income groups included in the project. In many cases this probably means that richer families are either directly allocated better located plots at the across-the-board price, or subsequently are able to exchange their plot, with some payment, for a better located one. In either case this would mean that subsequent locational profits from land and property value appreciation would be passed on to higher income groups.

Directly related to the plot/core options available and the pricing policy in a project are the respective repayment arrangements. The availability of appropriate credit in the forms of hire purchase or mortgages, and appropriate collection techniques, is vital to project success. Indeed, the project sales promotion and credit facilities together form the mechanism for a rapid uptake of plots and a reliable programme of repayment. When plot sizes and core house designs are not sensitive to customers' needs, or when credit arrangements are inadequate, financial losses will result from slow recruitment of families from the target group, from defaults on repayments by financially distressed families, or from the abandonment of plots by such families. The importance of designing repayment arrangements that are viable from the families' point of view in their new housing situation cannot be overstressed.

5.5 Sources of Funding

Funding to the agencies implementing the reviewed projects came predominantly from the respective national governments themselves. In four projects all capital for project implementation came from a direct government grant. Five project implementing agencies received total project funds in the form of a loan from their respective government, whilst the remaining agencies received funding partly in the form of a direct grant and partly as a loan. Significantly, in cases where implementing agencies received funding in the form of a loan they attempted to collect initial downpayments from incoming residents. However, it cases where the housing agencies were using finance from direct grants they made no such endeavours.

World Bank loans assisted five projects whilst one project was assisted by the Asian Development Bank (ADB) and the United States Agency for International Development (USAID).

For the Arumbakkam project, the government of Tamil Nadu was the recipient of a World Bank loan which it directed as a grant, together with state and national funds, to the Tamil Nadu Housing Board. These funds were provided on a grant basis to enable the TNHB to set up a revolving fund from cost recoveries to finance continuing sites and services projects. In several countries,

housing agencies themselves can take up loans directly from the international agencies, with the national government underwriting them. This is so in the case of Thailand, for example. In its Tung Song Hong project, the NHA of Thailand, with the approval of the National Economic and Social Development Board (NESDB), received a loan from the World Bank which, together with the funds from the Ministry of Finance, financed the project. Similarly, for the Bang Plee Bang Bor project, the NHA received direct loans from ADB and USAID. In some other countries, the agency is not authorized to take up such loans directly and it has to receive them indirectly, through state or national governments, as in the case of the Arumbakkam project. In national contexts, such as Thailand and the Philippines, where international funding can be initiated or sought by the relevant housing agency and, eventually, directly taken up by it, the agency is in a somewhat better position to influence its national government to ensure an increased flow from external financial resources to housing programmes.

5.6 Case Study Focus

The Arumbakkam project in Madras is appropriate for consideration in this chapter because it has been quite skilfully planned to achieve cost recovery as far as possible. It uses differential land pricing to enable cross subsidization for its large proportion of EWS plots. The project has been supported by the World Bank, and one of its design goals is to create a revolving fund to finance future sites and services schemes.

Case Study VII ARUMBAKKAM, MADRAS

(I) Urban Context

In 1901, the city of Madras had a population of about 550,000, which by 1941 had increased to some 880,000. During the 1940s the city had a good water supply system and most of its area was sewered. It was still primarily an administrative and commercial centre. Since independence, however, the city has grown rapidly, and in 1971 covered an area of 129 square kilometres with a population of about 2.5 million. The Madras Metropolitan Area (MMA), which covers about 1,170 square kilometres, had a 1971 population of 3.5 million, increasing at about 4 per cent annually. The present population (November 1981 is estimated at about 5.0 million to which over 200,000 are added annually.

Over the past 30 years a large number of public sector enterprises have been located in Madras, including the Integral Coach Factor, Madras Refinery and Fertilizers, and the Heavy Vehicles Factory. The Madras port has been expanded to an annual capacity of about 7.0 million tons of throughput. As well, a fisheries port has been constructed to accommodate 150 trawlers and

500 small boats. Many private sector companies have been attracted to the city, including Ashok Leyland and Standard Motors. Most major banks and stock companies of South India have situated their head offices in Madras. Nevertheless, most employment is in smaller establishments to which the Government of Tamil Nadu (GTN) is giving particular attention and support. New manufacturing ventures usually locate north and west of the city centre, while the expansion of trade and commerce is taking place in the centre itself and towards the south.

Average annual per capita income in the MMA in 1970–1971 averaged Rs 855 (US$95.00) which was considerably less than the per capita income in many other metropolitan areas in India. About 56 per cent of the total income is derived from the tertiary sector and 39 per cent from the secondary sector. Though unemployment statistics are unreliable, according to the 1971 census the work force participation rate in the Madras area was only about 28 per cent compared with 37 per cent in Bombay and 33 per cent in Calcutta.

Madras has serious deficiencies in important urban services with levels of services deteriorating. Water supply averages less than 70 litres per capita per day (lcd) though many domestic consumers, particularly in the poorest areas, receive less than 40 lcd. In transport, pedestrians and cyclists account for close to half of all person-trips, but facilities for them have been neglected and road investments have benefited mainly motor vehicle traffic.

The provision of serviced land and housing has not kept up with needs, particularly those of low income groups. The slum population of Madras has been increasingly more rapidly than has the overall city population and it now accounts for over 30 per cent of the total population, or about 1.2 million persons.

An intensive survey of slums carried out in the city in 1970 identified about 1,200 slums with a total population of about 740,000 persons, of whom an estimated 200,000 lived outside the city boundary in MMA. Existing GTN programmes in the housing sector have been primarily aimed at middle income groups and are beyond the affordability of the EWS. Programmes to alleviate the plight of the slum population have until recently emphasized slum clearance and resettlement at high cost in subsidized units rather than slum improvement. The primary approach adopted by the Tamil Nadu Slum Clearance Board (TNSCB) was to clear slums and house their populations in four-storied tenements constructed on the cleared site. Whilst the recent average cost per tenement unit was Rs12,500 (US$1,400), the monthly rental charges of Rs10 (US$1.15) recovered less than 10 per cent of the cost of construction, maintenance, and other overheads. At peak productivity the TNSCB provided only 3,500 units per year. Unit costs under the Madras Urban Development Programme—1 (MUDP—1) average about Rs5,670 (US$750), and the programme's annual provision of 3,000 units meets only 17 per cent of new EWS demand. The total annual deficit between all formal supply (including MUDP—1) and the need is about 20,000 units. This gap is typically met through new construction on unserviced land, the further overcrowding of existing slums, and subletting in new housing colonies.

The initiation of the sites and services and slum improvement programme under MUDP—1, which now affects about 10,000 households annually, introduced an effective two-pronged strategy for providing improved shelter and related services for the lowest income groups. Under the World Bank financed slum improvement programme, the average costs amount to only Rs1,300 (US$145) per household, of which 78 per cent is being recovered. Although MUDP—1 is now ensuring that the total number of households living in unserviced slums does not increase, it is still insufficient to overcome the existing backlog. The Arumbakkam sites and services project is the first of three such projects undertaken in MUDP—1.

(II) The Target Population for Arumbakkam Sites and Services

This project aimed at providing serviced land and housing particularly for families whose monthly incomes are less than Rs350 (US$40). It also aimed to provide them with health and education facilities, improved community environments and employment opportunities. The total target population numbered 2,300 families from various low income groups, of which nearly 1,700 families, or 74 per cent of the total, are from the EWS. Plot sizes and on-plot development have been designed with due consideration of the present living conditions of these poor urban families and their ability to pay.

(III) Site Selection, and Land Acquisition and Improvement

The land utilized for the Arumbakkam project is situated 9 kilometres to the west of the city centre in an area where slums have developed and where new industries and middle and high income group housing schemes are located.

There were a variety of reasons for selecting this site for the first sites and services scheme of MUDP—1. In the first place, it is located in a pressure area where a demand from the EWS target group had already been identified. It is well located for employment opportunities in terms of industrial development and higher income group residential areas. It is well connected to the city in terms of transport, and is soon to be accessible from the city centre and other surrounding economically active areas through construction of the MMA Inner City Ring Road.

Project land was mainly the property of the Madras Corporation (31.5 hectares), but a small segment (0.72 hectares) was in private ownership. The Madras Corporation had kept the land vacant in anticipation of using it to house its employees. The Madras Corporation had to be compensated and the privately owned portion was purchased. The acquisition of the land did not pose real problems, though the amount of compensation due to the Madras Corporation and the issue of preferential allotment to its employees within the scheme did require careful negotiation. Although the site was fairly level, some earth filling was required for low-lying pockets to achieve the level required by the project design. The cost of such land improvements was US$841 per hectare, including the cost of the design and supervision.

(IV) Infrastructural Development and Land Use

The internal network of streets and pedestrian circulation has been designed to connect with the network of adjacent residential settlements and transportation routes (see site plan). The project site is linked with P.H. Road, a main east–west artery of Madras, 600 metres to the north of the site, by a newly constructed access road, 15 metres in width. Two other major roads run east to west, in the north and south sections. Between these runs a spine road from north to south.

The layout design provides for various sectors of residential development, with secondary roads of 9 and 6 metres widths skirting the sectors. The streets within the sectors are of 6 and 3 metres in width. The standards and specifications were purposely below municipal regulations to restrain project costs in accordance with the incoming residents' ability to pay (see Table 7, p.68).

Land utilized for residential purposes amounts to 14.8 hectares, or 45.9 per cent of the total site area. Circulation accounts for 8 hectares, or 24.8 per cent of the project land (see Table 6, p.67).

Water supply for the project is provided by the Madras Metropolitan Water Supply and Sewerage Board. The site was linked to the MMWSSB main off site by laying 1,000 metres of 250 millimetres diameter cast iron main. Water is drawn into a sump of 1.6 million litres capacity and pumped to an overhead tank of 0.8 million litres capacity. The daily requirements of water for this scheme is 2.49 million litres, the demand being 135 lcd. All materials used for the water supply system conform to Indian Standard Specifications. Individual connections are available on the plots.

Masonry drains have been provided for the main roads with manholes provided at intervals of not more than 45 metres. Reinforced concrete slab open culverts have been provided for all other roads on the site.

The water-borne sewerage system has been designed for a minimum velocity of 0.6 metres per second. Cast iron pipes are used for house connections and stoneware pipes of 800 millimetres diameter have been laid for the mains. The sewage is pumped to a nearby sewage farm by means of the pumping station constructed on site.

The electricity supply network at Arumbakkam was installed by the Tamil Nadu Electricity Board (TNEB) and a total of 9 kilometres of cables were laid. The TNEB provides a metered supply to householders and manages the collection of consumption charges. Plot owners apply to TNEB and obtain individual connections on payment of connection fees. The Madras Corporation has provided 197 street lights which it maintains.

In designing this project, the extent of land for community facilities was based on actual needs rather than on existing planning standards. Eventually

104

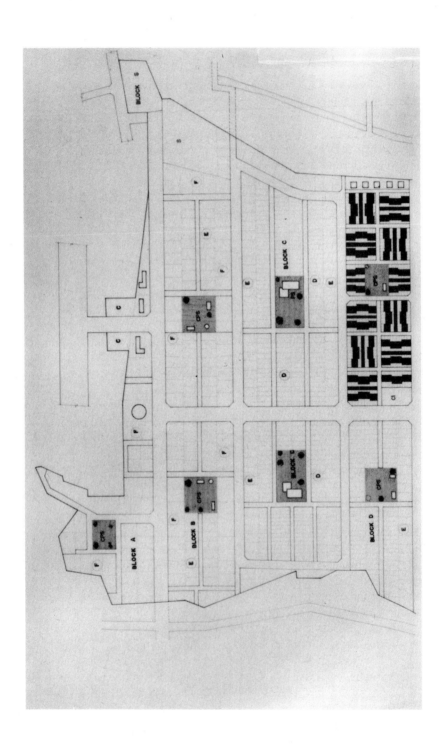

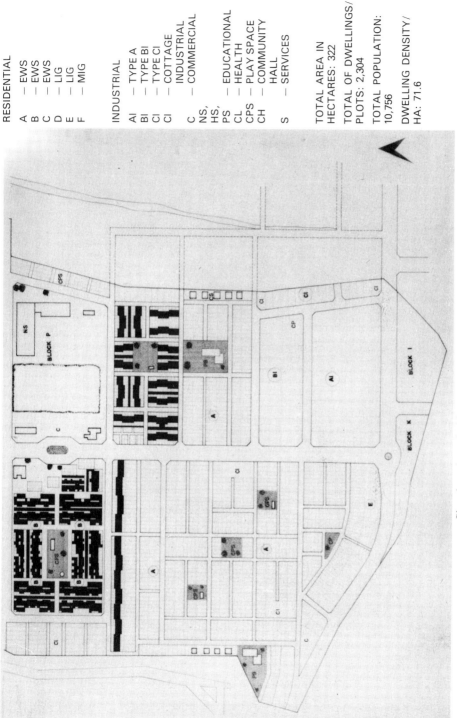

RESIDENTIAL

A — EWS
B — EWS
C — EWS
D — LIG
E — LIG
F — MIG

INDUSTRIAL

AI — TYPE A
BI — TYPE BI
CI — TYPE CI
CI — COTTAGE
      INDUSTRIAL
C — COMMERCIAL
NS,
HS, — EDUCATIONAL
PS — HEALTH
CL — PLAY SPACE
CPS — COMMUNITY
CH — COMMUNITY
       HALL
S — SERVICES

TOTAL AREA IN
HECTARES: 322

TOTAL OF DWELLINGS/
PLOTS: 2,304

TOTAL POPULATION:
10,756

DWELLING DENSITY/
HA: 71.6

Site plan: Arumbakkam project, Madras

Arumbakkam: open drainage reduced infrastructure costs

the project will include a high school, four primary schools, seven nursery schools, a clinic, a community hall, and facilities like a police station and post office. The total land required for these facilities is 2.1 hectares or 6.5 per cent of the total site area.

Commercial and industrial plots are also available within the project. For industrial use 2.0 hectares was allocated, and 2.8 hectares for commercial purposes, making a total 14.9 per cent of the site area.

(V) Plot and Shelter Development Options

There are five plot sizes which, with varying degrees of on-plot development, provide a total of six options. (See diagrams showing plot options.)

Arumbakkam: open drain culverts at road crossing

For EWS households, two plot sizes and three different types of cores have been designed in order to accommodate the relatively wide range of incomes in this category. The designs of the plots are dictated by the ability to pay of the target population. It is assumed that payments of 10–20 per cent of monthly income would be affordable by the lower to low-middle income groups.

Option 1 is a plot of 40 m² (13′ × 33′), with a sanitary core constructed with a brick wall and a roof of reinforced concrete and located at the rear of the plot. Each core contains a water closet and a bath with a tap. Cores are grouped by units of four. It was envisaged that the purchaser first sets up a thatched hut on the plot. Later, with the help of building materials provided by the project, this hut can be improved gradually, and eventually can become a house entirely built of durable materials. The monthly payment required for

108

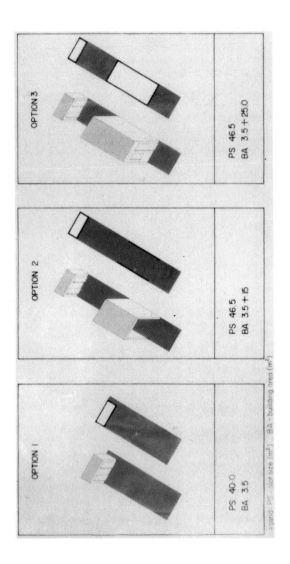

OPTION 1   OPTION 2   OPTION 3

PS 40·0   PS 46·5   PS 46·5
BA 3·5   BA 3·5 + 15   BA 3·5 + 25·0

PS – plot size (m²)   BA – building area (m²)

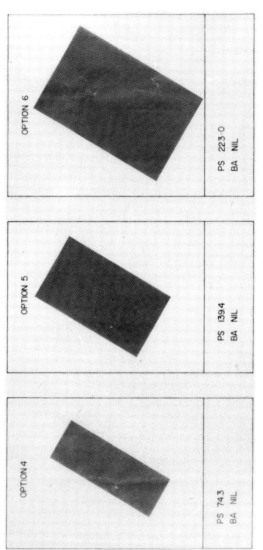

Plot options: Arumbakkam project, Madras

the plot and the superstructure is Rs22 per month, which was expected to attract households with incomes of Rs150–200 per month.

Option 2 is a plot of 46.5 m^2 (10′ × 50′). The superstructure includes a sanitary core, bath with a tap and wc, two 22 cm thick and 5 m long brick walls covered by a roof slab. Originally, it was proposed to provide a thatched roof but, on discussions held with the would-be beneficiaries, this was changed to roofing with partially precast beams and concrete blocks so that it is possible to add a first floor (see photographs) and to ensure that the structure would be fire proof. The covered area is 21 m^2. The first step to improve the house is to build front and back walls and possibly expand the ground floor, or to add a first floor with building materials provided by the project and also from private resources. A shop facing the street can be added in front of the house. The monthly payment required for the plot and the superstructure is Rs33 per month, which was expected to attract households with incomes of Rs200–300 per month.

Option 3 consists of a plot of 46.5 m^2 with a sanitary core and a super-structure including two rooms of 10.5 m^2 each. Plots are arranged in cluster form. The walls are 22 cm thick and constructed of bricks laid in cement mortar. The roof is made with partially precast beams and a solid concrete slab. The floor consists of rammed earth with cow dung finish. A shop of workshop can be added in front of the plot, and the walls and foundation have been designed to withstand another floor. The monthly payment required is Rs70 per month which could be afforded by a household with an income of Rs300–350 per month.

It should be noted that the target income groups for options 4, 5, and 6 are higher because there is no housing provided and it is anticipated that they will have to have higher incomes to finance the complete construction of their houses.

Option 4 consists of a plot of 74.3 m^2 with electricity, water, and sewerage connections. The repayment of loans is Rs45 per month which could be afforded by an LIG household with an income of Rs350–450 per month.

Option 5 consists of a plot of 139.4 m^2 with electricity, water and sewerage connections. The monthly payment required for the plot is Rs85 which could be afforded by an MIG household with an income of Rs450–600 per month.

Option 6 consists of a plot of 223.0 m^2 with electricity, water, and sewerage connections. The monthly payment required for the plot is Rs270 which could be afforded by an HIG household with an income of Rs600–1,000 per month.

(VI) Allocation and Tenure Conditions

The availability of plots in this project was announced in the daily press in the local language in order to attract the attention of the lower middle class and the economically weaker section of the community. Application forms were sold at nominal cost at selected centres throughout the city.

There were specific policies for the allotment of EWS plots (options 1, 2 and

3) and for the LIG/MIG/HIG plots (options 4, 5, and 6). The EWS plots were allotted as follows: 20 per cent for scheduled castes and tribes, 5 per cent for service industry employees; 5 per cent for tradesmen (masons, carpenters, etc.); and the remaining 70 per cent for unrestricted selection by families from the EWS income group. The LIG/MIG/HIG plots were allotted as follows: 20 per cent for scheduled castes and tribes; 10 per cent for state and central government employees; 10 per cent for implementing agencies employees; and the remaining 60 per cent for unrestricted selection by families from the respective income levels.

An allotment committee was formed at the MMDA consisting of representatives of various state government agencies directly or indirectly involved in the planning and implementation of the project. Applications received were processed according to guidelines prescribed by the allotment committee, which included stipulations concerning the calculation of family incomes and the specific eligibility of certain low-level Madras Corporation personnel.

Lots were cast for the allotment. The exact plot number was also decided by selected allottees casting lots. In anticipation of dropouts after selection, 30 per cent of the remaining cases under each category were also selected by the same method and kept on a waiting list according to the order of selection. After the selection, the allottees have to make an initial payment and sign their lease-cum-sale agreement to take over the plots.

The main features of the lease-cum-sale agreement executed with incoming residents are:

1 The occupant shall not assign or sublet without formal permission from the MMDA.
2 The occupant shall construct a building within 1 year.
3 The occupant shall not sell or otherwise dispose of the plot for 5 years. If the occupant does wish to sell or otherwise dispose of the plot the first offer must be to the lessor.
4 In case of defaults on repayments, the allotment is liable to cancellation.
5 The occupant can sell after 5 years and after receiving the sale deed.
6 A second mortgage is allowed before issue of sale deed after paying the land cost in full.

Industrial and commercial plots are allocated by a committee consisting of officials of the Small Industries Development Corporation (SIDCO), the MMDA, and the Tamil Nadu Housing Board. Applications received from the entrepreneurs are scrutinized and a selection is made by the committee. Plots are handed over after 25 per cent of the total cost has been paid to SIDCO.

The local market contains 39 small shops and 12 open plots which are allotted on a rental basis to EWS residents to generate employment. The 19 shophouses were auctioned as they are in a very attractive commercial location at the centre of the project site.

Arumbakkam: (top) factory in industrial zone; (bottom) recently auctioned shophouses in the central section

(VII) Financial Arrangements

The project was partially funded by a central government of India loan, by a direct budgeting allocation from the government of Tamil Nadu, and by a World Bank loan. The World Bank loan accounts for 50 per cent of the total

Arumbakkam: Community Hall

project costs. The World Bank released this amount to the government of India, which in turn released the funds to the government of Tamil Nadu for allocation to the various agencies implementing project components. In India, international development aid funds must be channelled through the central government. The revenue realized from plot and land sales is deposited in a revolving fund set up by the Tamil Nadu Housing Board. The fund was established in 1978 and is maintained separately for financing sites and services schemes.

There was no subsidy involved in any stage in the project. Complete recovery of costs is being achieved through a number of strategies.

Costs of land, land development, and on-site infrastructure are recovered through the sale of developed plots for residential, commercial, and industrial purposes. The differential pricing of marketable lands for various uses allows the provision of a cross subsidy within the scheme itself. The cost of land for EWS plots is only nominal at Rs1.00 per square metre but the subsidy is recouped by suitably pricing the industrial, commercial, and middle income group plots. However, care is taken that the pricing of industrial, commercial, and middle income group plots is at the prevailing market rates. The pricing structure is set out in Table 13.

Costs of on-plot developments are fully charged to the respective categories of beneficiaries. The recovery of costs incurred for off-site infrastructure (excluding access roads) by taxes and user charges is still under consideration.

The question of recovering costs incurred on community facilities is still under negotiation. The sites for these community facilities had been priced at a

Table 13 Pricing structure of plots in Arumbakkam

Plots	Original average price, US$/m² (1978)	Current price, US$/m² (1981)
Residential options 1, 2, & 3	0.125	0.125
option 4	5.625	5.625
option 5	5.625	6.250
option 6	5.625	6.875
Community facilities	3.750	6.250
Local commercial	5.625	12.500
Central commercial	10.625	12.500
Small industrial	11.250	11.250
Community Hall	11.250	6.250

higher rate to provide cross subsidy for EWS plots. This resulted in some reluctance by the private and public agencies concerned to take over these lands. So far the high school and two primary schools with their buildings constructed have been handed over to GTN and the Madras Corporation for operation, but without a final decision about who is to pay the costs. Due to similar difficulties, the post office was allotted to one of the shop-cum-residences and the clinic was rented out to a voluntary agency. In view of the above experience the entire pricing structure is being reworked to see whether the sites set apart for such purposes could be priced at half of their development value or even donated. However, it was decided that the cost of on-plot construction should be recovered from private or public agencies without any subsidy. In the case of school facilities, it was felt that the construction could be programmed in future in such a way that it will start when the settlers move in, or after a substantial number of settlers have moved in. Until such time, the schools could be housed in temporary sheds. This would avoid losses on investments resulting from the construction of schools well before the settlers move in.

The collection of application fees and initial deposits is carried out by the Superintending Engineer's Office of the TNHB. The collection of monthly repayments is being handled by bill collectors who approach the allottees directly. All collection is monitored by the Administrative Office of the Accounts Department of the Superintending Engineer's Office.

If any allottee falls into arrears in his repayments by more than two months, notice under the provisions of the Tamil Nadu Housing Board Act is served, and action is taken to cancel the allotment and evict the allottee from the plot if it is occupied. However, the bill collectors regularly warn allottees whose payments are in arrears before official notice is several. If a defaulting allottee has his allotment cancelled he is given one month to pay the entire arrears or make an appeal. If the entire amount is paid, the allotment is restored after a restoration fee of Rs75 has been paid. So far (1981) the rate of collection has been extremely satisfactory. An average repayment rate of 95 per cent has been achieved. Efforts are being made to maintain the same tempo in future. In

Arumbakkam: (top) extended unit (option 1), right, and extension (option 2) in progress, left. (Bottom) extended unit (option 2), right; original option, centre; and extension in progress, left

order to streamline collection procedures, it is proposed to computerize the entire collection system.

Financial arrangements have been made for loans to assist EWS allottees in their house construction and extension activities. Nationalized banks are providing the loans. Families who have taken up plot options 1 and 2 are given a bank loan to a maximum of Rs3,000, and families who have taken up plot

Arumbakkam: option 2 houses for EWS in various stages of development

option 3 are given a bank loan to a maximum of Rs2,000. The interest rate charged is 4.5 per cent for scheduled castes and scheduled tribes. Other categories are charged 12.9 per cent. The loans are repayable in 102 monthly instalments and the loan is a character loan given without any legal security.

The Communty Development Wing of TNHB helps the residents in getting the necessary application forms from the bank, taking the residents to the bank, and bringing bank officials to make an inspection on-site so the loan can

Arumbakkam: option 2 extended with a (temporary) upper floor (see also cover picture)

be sanctioned. Also, they help the bank by persuading the residents to make repayments by the due date.

(VIII) Maintenance

No maintenance charge is collected from the residents at Arumbakkam. Allottees have to maintain their houses and plots themselves. The Madras Corporation will periodically assess the houses erected by the residents and charge local taxes accordingly. Similarly, the Madras Metropolitan Water Supply and Sewerage Board will make water and sewerage charges. Both these organizations had not yet finalized such assessments in 1981.

Of the project infrastructure, the roads, drains, street lights, parks, playgrounds, etc., have been handed over to the Madras Corporation for maintenance. Similarly, the water supply system and sewerage system have been handed over to MMWSSB for maintenance.

Two difficulties arose in Arumbakkam while handing over the infra-structure for maintenance. The first problem was that the project had adopted specifications for minor roads (3 and 5 foot metres widths) which did not satisfy corporation standards which specify that there should not be any roads of less than 6 metres in width. However, in view of the project goals and the income levels of the beneficiaries, the corporation finally agreed to maintain all project roads.

The second problem was that the MMWSSB refused to take over maintenance of internal sewerage lines and water supply lines because these lines pass through private property. However, after protracted negotiations, the MMWSSB reluctantly agreed to take over these lines on the condition that future sites and services schemes should modify this method of supplying service connections.

Chapter 6

Evaluating Project Performance

6.1 Reaching the Intended Target Groups

The housing delivery system (or the way in which housing is made available in whatever form to whatever income level) is dynamic and the relationship between the supply of housing to one income group and the supply to another is symbiotic. From the demand side, in a context where the urban population growth rate is 5 per cent per annum, housing shortages are not restricted to the poor. In such a context it is impossible to undertake the delivery of housing (even in the limited forms implicit in the sites and services strategy) to one income group without having some direct impact on the delivery to other income groups. This is especially true where the macro-economic environment is left untouched by structural changes of any kind. The reviewed sites and services projects were clearly operating in this predicament and, consequently, any assessment of their overall performance in reaching target groups must take this into account. Furthermore, the tendency to relate to centralized construction tasks was carried over in the staffing and structure of implementing agencies (see section 6.2). Market mechanisms and speculation cannot be ignored and consequently the efficiency of the strategy and the success of individual projects have to be examined in the pervasive environment of those market laws and such speculation. It would be considerably different (though not necessarily better in net result) if similar projects were being evaluated in contexts where fundamental structural changes had been undertaken with regard to rural development, urban and rural land ownership, building materials production, and income distribution.

Among the ten implemented projects, the Arumbakkam, Dakshinpuri resettlement, and Dasmariñas projects showed considerable success in reaching their target groups which were predominantly comprised of very low income families. In the Arumbakkam project this success was mainly due to the careful planning that went into the project, specifically in realistically calculating the target group's ability to pay and matching it effectively to plot, core house, and infrastructural design and cost. The Dakshinpuri resettlement project also restrained standards of infrastructure and on-plot provision to retain affordability to its target groups, though more than half the recruited families categorized as eligibles (see case study IV, chapter 3) had their

119

payments subsidized by 50 per cent. Dasmariñas, which, like Dakshinpuri, recruited dislocated squatters and slum dwellers, used stringent income criteria to sieve out non target group families, but the project does involve significant subsidies which may lead to increased resale in the long run.

The Indonesian projects are somewhat unique in so far as the standard Perumnas policy of allocating the project plots primarily to civil servants directly distorts any comparison with other projects in other countries where this is not done. The outstanding project of the three was the Simomulyo resettlement project in Surabaya which resettled an existing community and which was exempted from this policy. (See case study VI, chapter 4.) In this project a successful matching of project design and implementation to target group needs was achieved.

Projects like the Metroville I project and the Rangsit project, which both had serious misallocation records, failed for a variety of reasons not specifically related to the sites and services strategy itself. Other projects achieved initial success in reaching their target groups but subsequently had difficulties in retaining them. This was primarily caused by inappropriate use of subsidies. As is to be expected whenever projects substantially subsidize residents, there have been high incidences of resale despite various regulations to prevent it. In the Vashi project, for example, where the Economically Weaker Section and Low Income Groups were substantially subsidized, about 40 per cent of houses have been resold. Predominant problems in reaching target groups were lack of knowledge of the market, lack of experience in designing and implementing such projects, and deficiencies in the organization set up for doing so.

The National Housing Authority of Thailand, for example, had formerly confined itself to heavily subsidized, centralized flat construction projects and had made little adjustment in terms of organization and personnel when it embarked on its Rangsit project. The authority indicated that it failed to reach its target group because the project's remote location and rigid core house design held little appeal for the planned target group households whose income per month was US$75. However, the subsequent steps of opening up the project to all income groups seemed to be related to the authority's desire to get results in terms of occupied core house units rather than to its planning priorities. Before reviewing other problems experienced in this area it is worth considering the discrepancies between planned target groups and actual market demand for the kind of housing opportunities that sites and services projects offer.

In the cities in which the reviewed projects were undertaken it is clear that the demand for housing from not only the low income groups but also from middle and even higher income groups was not being satisfied by the private sector. Consequently, there was inevitably competition from these other income groups for the housing opportunities being offered in the sites and services projects. This was especially so when the standards were commensurate with those of housing being sold on the open market by the private sector.

Such a tendency was further exacerbated when projects offered subsidies which, of course, the private sector never does.

The need for thorough market research, that embraces the existing supply and standards of housing from public, private, and popular (or informal private sector as seen in slum communities whether rental or squatter) sectors and the demand from all income groups, is vital to an understanding of from where applications and competition for housing opportunities that might be offered in sites and services projects will come. Only when this knowledge is available can projects be realistically designed to reach and retain specific target groups that are not being catered for by other housing suppliers from the private or public sector. The Thai experience in sites and services has been the subject of attention in a recent study of the housing market, and the following passage explains how the existing market conditions directly affect demand for sites and services housing opportunities.

> From the results of the housing market survey it appears that the real client group for NHA sites and services would be households with income between 2,000 bahts to 8,000 bahts per month. But because of the project location (e.g. Bang Plee Bang Bor, Lad Krabang) on the urban fringe of the city, most of the demand will come from households with incomes above 3,000 bahts per month (84% of applicants in Tung Song Hong sites and services project had incomes above 3,000 bahts per month and 48% had income above 4,000 bahts). Within the context of the present housing market and because of the current gap in the provision of housing finance to middle income groups, households with income around 4,000 bahts per month, are as worthy of NHA attention as households with income of 2,500 bahts. But because of the location and standards of present sites and services it is probable that many more households in the 4,000 bahts income range will apply for NHA plots than households with income around 2,500 bahts. If the NHA wants to keep the emphasis on target groups below the 30th percentile households with income below 3,500 bahts, it is clear that some revision of both *location* and *standards* of projects should be made. (National Housing Authority of Thailand, 1980)

Whilst the revision of standards is possible, the availability of locations that are more attractive to low income families, and that they can afford, is questionable as long as speculation in city land prices continues in cities like Bangkok.

Unfortunately, the method most commonly employed to prevent other income groups from intruding into sites and services projects is the screening process. Screening processes are seldom reliable and often contribute to corrupt practices at one level or another. Even if they are relatively effective in the initial allocation of plots, they are likely to be circumvented later by clandestine resale to families of higher income levels than the planned target group. Such higher income families can more easily survive the economic strain resulting from relocation and can better perceive the long-term investment value of housing opportunities available in the project.

An appropriate way to offset this trend is to augment the supply of housing to other income groups through other means. This would necessarily involve stimulating the private sector to deliver housing that is more affordable to an income level that is not the target of government low income housing projects. A direct means of doing this would be to lower prevailing standards and regulations so as to enable private sector developers to deliver cheaper housing whilst still retaining attractive profit margins. Certainly, the probable increase in the delivery of housing units could help them maintain an overall profit margin despite reductions in profit per unit. Also there is the possibility of revamping financing mechanisms to assist would-be home owners from these income groups. It may also be appropriate to give tax incentives to private developers to produce more housing units for these income groups. Efforts could also be made to develop the building materials industry so that cost and supply constraints resulting from its current limitations could be removed. Certainly, a strong argument can be made to convince the private sector that the scale of demand for housing lies not in the upper percentile income groups but rather in the vast numbers from middle and lower percentiles.

At the project design level it is possible to limit the degree to which non-targeted income groups compete for sites and services plots by using standards that are less attractive to such income groups. Alternatively, projects can be designed to include housing for such other income levels at differential standards, competitive with the private sector. But the history of housing agencies does not augur well for such adjustments, because of their in-appropriate organizational structure and because of the professional, attitudinal, and moral limitations of some of their personnel (see below).

6.2 Agency Ability to Design and Implement Sites and Services

Sites and services projects, despite their conceptual divergence from conventional construction programmes, still have to sustain the burden of the organization or agency involved, and this is reflected in construction costs. If the structure of the organization involved in designing and implementing the project is deficient, then, regardless of the suitability of the strategy or the quality of the personnel, projects cannot attain their goals. The cooperative search for reasoned solutions to practical problems through a meaningful role within an organizational context degenerates into frustrating and inefficient conflicts over control. These conflicts distort perceptions of the problems and the preoccupation with control reduces the flexibility of the organization to derive and apply solutions.

A major and common problem in many of the project agencies is the excessive number of hierarchical levels in the structure of the agency combined with centralized decision making. As a result of this, authority in the form of decision making is exercised by someone who is not directly responsible for and involved in carrying out the actions resulting from that decision. This prevents the vital flow of feedback from the respective field of activity in a project from reaching and influencing the decision making process. A case in which direct action was taken to overcome this was the Simomulyo resettlement project in Surabaya. The striking success in the rapid design and implementation of the project was due to the Manager making implementation decisions himself, often without waiting for the result of formal centralized decision procedures at the Jakarta head office. Decentralization in decision making makes for more rapid, cost effective project planning and implementation. Admittedly, it reduces the quantity of checks and balances in an organization, but generally the actual extent of centralization is so substantial that any move towards decentralization will have a favourable cost-benefit ratio.

Organizational deficiencies of the main agency concerned with a project are compounded when decisions are supposed to be taken in consultation with a number of other agencies which have similar problems of their own and which are sometimes reluctant to cooperate with each other. The Karachi Development Authority's Metroville I project depended heavily on external collaborating agencies such as the Karachi Metropolitan Corporation, the Department of Social Welfare, and the House Building Finance Corporation. In order to coordinate the different functions of these agencies, the Karachi Development Authority (KDA) formed the Metroville Executive Committee. However, higher-level decisions were unable to be made or expedited because of the reluctance of senior officers from different sections of the KDA and outside agencies to cooperate on basic implementation matters. Even when agreement was reached among senior officials it was still likely that actual execution would be frustrated by lack of cooperation at lower levels. Sometimes the structural deficiencies of agencies undertaking sites and services projects are aggravated by the attitudinal and behavioural shortcomings of their personnel. In some cases it is just a lack of commitment in doing one's job. Housing agencies are too often burgeoning organizations that provide security of employment for unenterprising professionals who have no commitment to any of the agency's declared goals. Corruption adds to the problem. The Metroville I project again provides a good example. A KDA official involved in the administration of Metroville I explained the difficulties that beset a society and bureaucracy when corruption is a way of life.

> We are doing our best to carry out this project as honestly as possible. But because the people have accepted corruption as a way of life, therefore, they hardly believe that things can go well without bribes — especially at the KDA. So, instead of choosing the right path — for sometimes there is genuine need to wait due to lack of technical staff or for some other constraints — the prefer to pay money and get rid of the problems . . . . I have opened my office to all the

allottees of Metroville in order to know directly about their problems and to solve them, if I can. But they tend to see the lower staff to resolve their problems in their own way. And, as you know, they are all human beings. (Siddiqui, 1980, p.23)

Obviously, project performance is adversely affected by such attitudes and practices. This demonstrates clearly the limitation in impact of individual projects, if the larger project environment is not attuned to performance.

6.3 Achieving Adequate Cost Recovery to Facilitate Replicability

The evolution of the sites and services approach has certainly helped to broaden government agency understanding of what housing arrangements are. In the course of designing and implementing projects, professionals in housing bureaucracies have had to dismantle old archetypes of housing delivery into basic components, viz. a plot of land; a range of separate services at a variety of standards relating to the physical and economic context; some minimal regulations governing how and where structures may be erected; and some supporting finance and income generation mechanisms to enable the household to acquire tenure right to the land and to finance the gradual development of its shelter. Breaking down the myth that housing has to be a completely finished, high-quality product has helped agencies to understand why their former conventional construction programmes did not and could not deliver housing to the vast numbers of urban poor. It has injected a dose of realism into the perception of the housing question and into urban planning as a whole. This has resulted in a turning away from imported models of city development and housing standards and stimulated housing research in the local context. This in turn has sharpened understanding of the resources available for housing action and of the techniques through which people from all income levels acquire housing.

The above observations raise the question of whether sites and services projects have proved to be more economical in their use of scarce resources and more effective in mobilizing the families' resources for the housing effort, so that low income housing stock can be produced on a large scale. The answer to the first part of the question, after examination of the case studies reviewed, is a rather positive one. This is particularly so in relation to government expenditure per unit and, to a lesser degree, in relation to cost recovery. The level of subsidy in sites and services is substantially lower than it had been previously in conventional housing schemes. Regarding mobilization of low income families' resources for the provision and development of their shelter, the record of sites and services is, generally speaking, a good one too: the fact is that, given time and a minimal level of economic security, families will gradually direct resources to housing in accordance with their individual capacity to do so.

The question of replicability via complete cost recovery, to facilitate provision of large-scale housing opportunity, is more complicated. Is it practicable and necessary for sites and services projects to attempt full cost recovery to achieve their goals? The practicability of doing so seems doubtful in view of the fact that so far none of the many sites and services projects assisted by the World Bank have achieved full cost recovery.

The necessity of doing so is also questionable. Some public spending has to be directed to the low income population through the provision of services and utilities and housing opportunities, just as it gets directed to middle and higher income groups through the provision of such services and utilities, as well as other urban developments such as roads, freeways, airports, and other prestigious public facilities from which the poor benefit very little. The issue really is how such public spending can be distributed to or spread across the largest possible number of families. Thus, in sites and services projects, minimizing subsidy is a real and achievable goal and it is a necessary (but not sufficient in itself) condition to enable replicability. What matters is to achieve levels of subsidy that are sustainable in the long run. In this regard the Arumbakkam project is faring well and the Gujaini project, in view of its thorough planning, has similar potential (see section 6.4 below).

Housing agencies in cities like Manila, Bangkok, and Madras are beginning to achieve some effective coordination between their ongoing slum improvement programmes and available plot or core house units in their current sites and services projects for overspill population from the slums undergoing improvement. In each case the families benefiting from the improvement programmes vastly outnumber those who take up plots in sites and services projects. It is both functional and feasible to achieve a sustainable proportion between the two activities. The provision of sites and services on a scale that could eventually substitute for slum improvement seems, however, to be unfeasible and even undesirable. It is unfeasible because of the obvious constraints in the agencies, and in the availability of resources, especially land, and because of the economic limitations of the large numbers of very poor families in slums and squatter communities. It is undesirable because it would effectively uproot and remove low income families from central and intermediate urban locations, probably adversely affecting their economic and social prospects. In view of these considerations it is perhaps better to evaluate the scale of sites and services projects in terms of their ability to facilitate effective large-scale slum improvement and slum reconstruction programmes.

6.4 Cost Recovery Performance

The collection of repayments for implemented projects, either in the form of rent or of instalments on mortgages or hire purchase agreements, ranged from 32 per cent in the Rangsit project to 97 per cent of the due amounts in the Metroville I project. However, both of these projects are not particularly helpful guides to predicting recovery performance for sites and services projects, because plots were predominantly allocated to households having higher incomes than the intended target group. More helpful indications come from the Vashi project and the Arumbakkam project where regular repayments were received from over 90 per cent of the projects' households. The Perumnas project in Medan reported successful repayment collection from over 90 per cent of project residents, but this was largely so because beneficiaries are predominantly civil servants and other employees having regular jobs. Their repayments are deducted at source from their salaries. The Dasmariñas project has so far managed to achieve due repayments from 60 per cent of its residents.

In several projects difficulties were encountered in establishing appropriate collection procedures, which pointed to the need to streamline such procedures in the future. Legal action against defaulting households was also difficult to carry out in practice, especially in cases where real economic hardship was the cause. Most projects have eviction clauses in their agreements with the households which they can legally apply. However, agencies found that it is difficult to apply such a measure without due analysis of the particular case. Some projects, like the Rangsit project and the Arumbakkam project, actually imposed fines on families who fell more than 2 months behind in their repayments.

Generally speaking, there is a definite need to tighten up collection procedures. Also, clear specific statements and instructions should be included in promotional pamphlets, and later in formal contracts, to provide an intelligible and credible enforcement process to deal with repayment default. Problems sometimes arise because client responsibilities are not clearly defined by the agency. Decentralized collection offices should be set up, which would be more accessible to residents, particularly if the hours of business of such offices are adaptable to the time constraints of the low income people in the projects. In fact, most implemented projects had used only one collection centre that operated only during conventional business hours. It appears that some further experimentation is possible with alternative collection methods. Apart from deductions at source (where this is applicable), utilization of post offices and banks to deposit repayments could be considered, as well as house to house collection, either by the agency or by the community itself (group collection).

While project experience has led to the general recognition that each case of payment delinquency needs to be looked at specifically and sympathetically, this experience has also made it clear that project agencies could not avoid carrying out eviction procedures in cases of hard core wilful delinquency.

6.5 Case Study Focus

The Dasmariñas Bagong Bayan project in Manila is a large-scale sites and services project specifically designed and implemented to accommodate squatters and other low income people dislocated from urban upgrading areas or from demolished slums. The project's extremely peripheral location and its very uniformly low income population have contributed to specific problems of employment opportunities, core house development, and repayment. Nevertheless, the implementing agency, the NHA of the Philippines, has demonstrated increasing awareness of such issues and earnestness to find suitable remedies for them.

Case Study VIII DASMARIÑAS BAGONG BAYAN, MANILA

(I) Urban Context

The population of Metropolitan Manila in January 1981 was about 7 million, or about 14.6 per cent of the country's 48 million people.* The city produces one third of the nation's Gross National Product and of all value added in secondary and tertiary activities.

It has the main international port handling 70 per cent of imports to the Philippines, and the only regularly operating international airport, and it is the centre of both higher education and cultural activity. Some 90 of the country's 100 biggest corporations, all major newspapers, all the commercial television stations, 60 per cent of all manufacturing establishments, and 45 per cent of the country's non-agricultural labour force are located in Metro Manila.

Metro Manila has to contend with the problems of inadequate housing, of the proliferation of squatter settlements and slums, and of poverty and unemployment. The urban population of the Philippines increases at a faster rate (currently 3.6 per cent per annum) than the pace at which initiated development controls can reap effective results. This particularly applies to Metro Manila where the current growth rate is 5 per cent. The squatter population accounts for 30–35 per cent of the entire population of Metro Manila.

In response to this undesirable situation, the government proposed a pattern of development geared to promoting growth centres on the extreme periphery of Metro Manila with strong development potentials for redistributing population and economic opportunities in the metropolitan region. Dasmariñas Bagong Bayan was identified as such a centre because of its location and because government land was available.

(II) Project Aims and Site Location

The Dasmariñas Bagong Bayan (DBB) sites and services project is a planned resettlement especially geared to developing a new community for evicted Manila squatters and low income families dislocated from urban upgrading areas. Incoming families are provided with serviced lots and, in later phases, core houses. Recognizing that providing a livelihood for incoming families is as important as the provision of housing opportunities, the National Housing

* Estimated from the 1980 census by the National Census and Statistical Office of the Philippines.

Authority planned the integrated development of Dasmariñas, complete with factories, a commercial centre, schools, a hospital, and all necessary life support systems.

The Dasmariñas resettlement area is located 28 kilometres south-west of Manila, along the Manila–Tagaytay Road. The 652 hectare site of gently rolling land is adequate to house 6,000 families. Initially, the resettlement project land consisted of 234 hectares that had been acquired in 1960, encompassing five disjointed areas. To arrive at a consolidated area and achieve a practical distribution of land use, the expropriation of private land around and between the disjointed parcels was necessary. This remaining area of 418 hectares was acquired in 1975 by the National Housing Authority.

The Dasmariñas site was specifically selected for model community planning because of its accessibility to Metro Manila as a result of improved communication and transportation facilities. Also, the area is strategically located in relation to other municipalities, which enhances its pivotal role in relation to the development of Cavite and other surrounding provinces.

Land improvement followed the terrain of the area. Land cut and fill were kept to a minimum. Disjointed areas were connected by opening roads and by bridge construction.

(III) Agency Involvement in Planning and Implementation

The development and administration of the project area is carried out by the National Housing Authority. Normally, the NHA sets its own project objectives and criteria for development. Whenever necessary, a private local planning firm is commissioned to undertake a study of the proposed project area, to prepare a general land use plan, and to recommend general planning considerations. The NHA Task Force on Relocation and Resettlement identifies target areas for relocation and undertakes census surveys of project beneficiaries in squatter and slum areas. Such information is then passed on to the Project Implementation Department to serve as a basis for detailed architectural and engineering design. Physical development is directly undertaken by the NHA.

The construction phase in Dasmariñas Bagong Bayan is principally handled by the Project Implementation Department. Construction projects are usually awarded through public tender and, in some instances, through negotiation. Contracts of less than 1 million pesos (US$150,000) are negotiated and those of more than 1 million pesos are publicly tendered. Once a contract has been awarded, the Project Manager calls for preconstruction conference to discuss in detail the mechanics of undertaking the contract.

During actual construction, the Project Engineer conducts a daily inspection of the project and prepares project documentation. Once a week, the Project Manager calls the contractors to a conference for performance assessment and to discuss problems encountered. Once the contract is completed, an Acceptance Committee is formed to conduct the final inspection and acceptance of the contract work.

When physical development has been completed, the project is turned over to the NHA-DBB Project Team for administration, after which the Project Team starts processing applications and accepting project participants. Socio-economic development components are arranged by the Project Team with support coming from the government and private agencies concerned. In order to avoid duplication of roles and to maximize delivery of services, socio-economic development components are integrated into a general framework plan jointly designed by the agencies comprising the interagency body. At mid-year and year-end, an evaluation of performance is undertaken. These then become references for the following year's general framework plan.

(IV) Infrastructural Development and Land Use

Circulation systems were designed to ensure safety and convenience while respecting existing life styles and stressing linkages between functional areas.

— Walkways between blocks of houses and adjacent functional areas have been designed to be strictly pedestrian. They are 4 metres wide.
— The pattern of pedestrian paths is in most cases direction and destination oriented. This results in an 'informal' radial pattern. Pedestrian walkways, 2 metres in width, along roads are segregated from all other modes of movement with shrubs and/or planting strips.
— Vehicular routes are segregated from pedestrian movement, except for minor roads. Local short-haul jeepneys and tricycles plying the routes between the bus stations and the residental and other activity areas are limited to the vehicular loops which encircle and service the entire resettlement area. Through traffic will not directly pass through the residential

Dasmariñas Bagong Bayan: a newly constructed walkway

Dasmariñas Bagong Bayan: walkway under construction in a newly occupied area of the project

zones. Passengers bound for areas outside the settlement have to walk or take connecting rides on short-haul public vehicles to the off-street loading and unloading zones that have been located at main complexes, where traffic is expected to be heavy. These zones reduce traffic loads on main streets and do not lead to bottlenecks. Where these zones are distant from buildings or covered areas, waiting sheds will be provided for the convenience of the commuters.

Most of the physical infrastructure for circulation is already operational except for the main bus terminal which still awaits development. Some 75.33 hectares have been utilized for circulation accounting for 16.65 per cent of the total site area.* (See Tables 6 and 7, pp.67 and 68, for comparative data on land use and circulation standards.)

Water supply is provided through the construction of deep wells with an average depth of 180 metres, each deep well having a submersible pump that can generate an average of 910 litres per minute. Each deep well is supplemented by a 270,000 litre elevated steel tank.

At present, there are nine deep wells and water tanks supplying water to the population. Additional water sources will be established as new zones in the settlement are occupied.

Water mains run along the major roads and pathways. A series of gate valves and fire hydrants are installed in strategic locations. Water points (housing block taps and laundry taps) are strategically situated throughout the

* Not counting designated open spaces.

Dasmariñas Bagong Bayan: communal water supply and laundry facility in a newly occupied area in the project

entire area to ensure even water distribution. A water point serves approximately 30–40 families. Water supply is confined to the communal system and there are no individual water connections. However, residents may eventually tap from the water mains at their own expense when the water supply facilities have been adequately developed.

Due to fluctuations in electric current, the motors of the water pump trip, thereby cutting off the water supply every now and then. When this happens, the water supply to the community is rationed. In order to avoid inconvenience to the residents, back-up artesian wells will be constructed.

Water administration is now being handled by the Dasmariñas Water Service Cooperative under the supervision of the National Housing Authority. Ultimately, autonomy will be given to the cooperative in running the affairs of the water system, covering both management and maintenance aspects.

In order to bring down development costs, minimum standards of development have been applied in Dasmariñas Bagong Bayan. The drainage system consists mainly of side ditches and open canals with only the industrial and commercial areas having an underground drainage and sewerage system.

Each family unit is provided with a sanitary core with a water sealed toilet and a septic tank. Effluents from residential sanitary cores drain to the open canals and ultimately to the natural waterways in the area.

Garbage disposal is mainly an individual family activity. Each family digs its own compost pit in the backyard. A system of proper garbage disposal has been introduced whereby only organic wastes are thrown into the compost pits and buried. Garbage like paper, cans, bottles, and plastic are collected and sold.

For the industries, a dumping site has been identified where industrial wastes are dumped and burned. Scrap materials which can be recycled are given to residents who make them into saleable items like pillows, doormats, dolls, etc.

Electricity is supplied by the First Cavite Electric Cooperative. Inc. (FCECI), which gets its current from the National Power Corporation, which was allowed a 30 metre right of way for its main power lines to traverse the southern portion of the resettlement area. Electricity poles and lines of the FCECI run along the major and secondary roads of the project area and along pathways in the residential areas. To date, all industries and 40 per cent of the residential areas are supplied with electricity. The FCECI will eventually establish a 15,000 kVA substation that will supply all the residential, commercial, and industrial power needs of the resettlement project.

The plans and design for energy supply are not included in NHA project development plans but are made by consultants for the FCECI. The result, therefore, is that electricity often comes some time after families have been resettled. To expedite the provision of electricity, the NHA has advanced funds to the FCECI in order that electrification of new residential areas can be undertaken as a priority. The cost of electricity consumption is a direct expense of the user. Street light costs are borne by the National Housing Authority.

The existing school programme available in Dasmariñas Bagong Bayan are at elementary, high school, and collegiate levels. However, vocational and informal programmes will be geared towards the development of skills to meet the projected demand for skilled labour in the area. A central high school, five elementary schools, and a private university constitute the formal education system in Dasmariñas Bagong Bayan. For a number of years, however, there were too few classrooms to accommodate the student population. In October 1981, this shortage of classrooms, both in the elementary and the high school levels, was finally met by the education authority's delivery of prefabricated classrooms. The families at Dasmariñas are young with a large number of school-age children, and the vast majority of families consider their children's education a high priority.

In the initial phases of the project, one rural health unit attended to the medical and health needs of the entire resettlement area. Later, a private foundation constructed, and now operates, a 200 bed hospital. Families from Dasmariñas receive treatment at a minimal fee. In addition to this service, two private universities send their respective medical and nursing students to render free medical and health services through the health outreach programme.

Community Development Council centres and/or spaces for such centres have been provided for every 500 to 1,000 families. A model centre was constructed by the NHA. The other centres were constructed by the community with technical and material assistance from the NHA. Areas for playgrounds have also been provided. The development of such areas is undertaken by the residents with technical and material assistance from the NHA.

A church constructed by the community is situated at the centre of the resettlement area. The increase in population and the opening of two new areas warrant the construction of additional chapels.

A branch post office set up in the area provides postal services for the entire community. To date, only the factories in the industrial estate have a telephone service.

A private transportation firm provides a regular bus service on the route between Manila and the project area route, but at a relatively high cost. A return trip amounts to almost 30 per cent of a minimum-wage worker's daily income. Another company operates minibuses to augment the bus service and the fares are slightly lower. Privately owned passenger jeepneys provide a service on the shorter Zapote–DBB route. Tricycles provide services within the resettlement project. Metro Manila Transit Corporation, a government controlled entity, is expected to start a bus service to augment the existing transportation services in the area.

The entire 652 hectare resettlement site has been divided into five major component areas: the residential zone, the industrial zone, the central business district, the institutional area, and open spaces. The residential area accounts for 56.8 per cent of the total project area (see Table 6, p.67).

The industrial zone accommodates two industrial estates, one located to the north and the other to the south of the project area. Industrial zones account for 43.8 hectares, or 9.7 per cent of the site area.

The institutional zone encompasses areas for the government centre hospital, elementary and high schools, university, sports complex, church, and cemetery. A total of 61.12 hectares, or 13.5 per cent of the site, is for these purposes.

The open spaces are defined areas which are either developed into parks or productive greening areas or maintained in a natural and undisturbed condition to enhance the quality of the environment.

(V) Dwelling Types, Allocation Procedures, and Terms of Sale

Initially, Dasmariñas Bagong Bayan offered only a 200 m^2 dwelling plot. In 1976, changes in policies and development concepts resulted in the provision of sanitary cores on smaller dwelling lots of 100 m^2. The resettled families would reconstruct their houses around this core. Later developments still utilized the smaller, 100 m^2 plot but introduced the construction of skeleton houses and/or complete shell houses in addition to the sanitary core.

Resettled families would then complete the housing units using whatever housing materials were salvaged after relocation. Both house types offered initial built areas of 30 m^2 and households were allowed to extend their dwellings towards the rear of their plots, which resulted in a maximum built-up area of 50 m^2. The front easement of 50 m^2 may not be built on.

Dasmariñas Bagong Bayan: rapid skeleton house development. This family moved in a week before the photograph was taken

Dasmariñas Bagong Bayan: skeleton houses in various stages of development in a newly occupied area

Additional housing materials were supplied to the project participants through the NHA's Housing Materials Loan Programmes and through the Freedom to Build project. The Freedom to Build project is a non-governmental organization which runs a building supply store providing a variety of

Dasmariñas Bagong Bayan: overview of a newly occupied (one week) area

Dasmariñas Bagong Bayan: an area being occupied. The construction of walkways and drains is still in progress

materials at prices considerably below Manila's commercial prices. It also supplies technical assistance.

The expansion of dwelling units as desired by the residents must be cleared with the National Housing Authority's site office.

Plots in Dasmariñas Bagong Bayan are generally intended for marginal income families dislocated from urban upgrading areas or relocated from other squatter colonies in Metro Manila. Families eligible for a plot are identified and recruited as follows. The NHA and the local government concerned undertake a census survey of squatter families of the particular area to determine who qualifies for resettlement. Subsequently, the NHA issues a clearance to the local government, authorizing them to proceed with the transfer of qualified squatters to Dasmariñas. Each family listed in the clearance is given one plot in the resettlement project.

Originally, the policy on land tenure in Dasmariñas was to provide leasehold for 25 years, renewable for another 25 years, but this was never implemented. After a review of the land tenure issue, the NHA adopted the policy of leasehold with an option to purchase at any time after resettlement. This policy came into effect in January 1981. When a household exercises the option to purchase, it can either pay the cost in full or amortize it over a period of 30 years at 12 per cent interest per annum. Lease payments made by the plot holder before exercising the option to purchase are credited against the principal of the selling price. Prior to full payment of the purchase price, the title to the lot is issued in the name of the beneficiary and the title is then mortgaged to NHA. Once full payment is made, mortgage is released and the cleared title is issued to the beneficiary. By 31 October 1981, 463 titles had been issued and another 207 titles were being processed.

Sales of home lots or ownership transfers have to be cleared and approved by the National Housing Authority.

(VI) Employment Generation

The NHA recognized that the provision of job opportunities was a fundamental ingredient for the success of this project. A major step towards achieving this goal was the development of the industrial zones. Factory buildings were constructed and industrial support systems were introduced including a 2 kilometre multilane highway, additional deep wells and reserve tanks for water, telephones, and a substantially improved electricity system. Total investment exceeded 20 million pesos. The industrial entrepreneurs were spared some capital investment because of these NHA inputs. Because Dasmariñas is a resettlement site, it is exempt from the ban on industries within 50 kilometres of Metro Manila. Entrepreneurs were also given tax privileges as incentives.

The industrial development to date consists of five large one-storey factory buildings (see photographs on pages 137 and 138). Four were provided by the NHA and one was built by the company itself. By January 1978, ten contracts with an employment potential of 5,000 jobs had been signed. Areas of employment included the manufacture of ladies' and children's wear, shoes, abrasives, and gloves as well as a large laundry. Some 75 per cent of the

Dasmariñas Bagong Bayan: factory building for garment production for export. The manufacturers are exempt from duty and taxes, but vulnerable to EEC restrictive practices

employment entails sewing garments for export,* implying a female work force. However, other small factories provide mixed employment. Initially, manufactures started operations on a limited scale but gradually moved towards full-scale production.

The NHA, in screening prospective entrepreneurs, did make inquiries about the projected level of employment, but concerned itself more with questions related to physical environment: water and electricity requirements, waste disposal, potential for air pollution, etc. There was no equivalent evaluation of the impact on the 'social environment', on wages, or the quality of employment to be provided. Contracts signed with the NHA put to constraints on managements as to wages or conditions of employment.[†] Whilst the NHA insists on its administrative control over the area, it is not able to review labour practices. The NHA Project Manager has, however, mediated in several labour disputes in the factories.

---

* The majority of industries produce purely for export under free trade zone conditions. The EEC is the largest market and this means that production levels and employment are extremely vulnerable to changes in EEC quotas. During 1980-1981, several factories were forced to reduce the number of shifts because of such restrictive practices.

† Employees of Atlas Gloves, Inc., and Berlie Hestia Ltd have to sign contracts with specified training periods of 2,500 hours and 2,800 hours respectively, and are paid approximately 9 pesos daily during the training period, which is below the already inadequate legal minimum wage of 13 pesos (in 1980). (It is unlikely that a person, presumably with an average degree of human dexterity and with 8 hours a day practice, would not be fully productive at a routine job after a month or so.) Furthermore, there are no constraints on employee turnover so the management could continue to operate indefinitely by rotating an underpaid trainee work force.

Dasmariñas Bagong Bayan: residents supply most of the labour to garment factories
site

Dasmariñas Bagong Bayan: employment in garment factories is mainly for young
females and does little to ameliorate unemployment among heads of households

Thus, if present trends continue, employees will remain at subsistence level
or below. Whereas adequate wages, generated and spent in the community,
would have a substantial multiplier effect and create other, secondary employment opportunities, wages trimmed to a survival level do not provide the
surplus necessary to create a healthy and diversified economic environment.

Besides the issue of inadequate wages there are three other observations that need to be made about the generation of employment opportunities in Damariñas. In the first place, there are not enough jobs available. A survey of employables conducted in 1979 revealed that 43.8 per cent were unemployed. Of those who were employed, 68.6 per cent worked in Metro Manila, 20.4 per cent worked in the industries and commercial centres in the project, and 11 per cent had jobs in the project's vicinity. The second point is that the impact of the factories is uneven and there is not a one-to-one correspondence between family needs and job opportunities with about 75 per cent of the openings being sewing jobs for young women, some families cannot participate at all. The third point is that a significant number of jobs were filled by existing employees from the companies' other installations or by more highly skilled and experienced workers from outside the area, mainly from Manila itself. In October 1981, 4,111 persons were employed in the factories on the site, out of which 60 per cent were area residents. NHA's declared target in this regard is 80 per cent, and whenever vacancies arise it insists that area residents are employed if their skills match those required for the job. Unfortunately, this is often not the case. Thus a situation persists whereby many unskilled or low-skilled residents commute daily (or weekly if they stay over during the working week) to Manila whilst skilled people living in Manila commute 30 kilometres or so to Dasmariñas to work.

In addition to these weaknesses in the contribution of the industrial estate to the viability of the community, there is a serious need to open and stimulate the operations of the commercial and business areas on the project site. So far, little development has taken place. In 1975 a market was erected and it has been periodically extended in accordance with the population growth of the project. Also, in 1979 a government sponsored Kadiwa department store was opened to supply a wide variety of retail items to the community.

(VII) Estate Management Issues

By January 1981, there had been 169 cases of plot abandonment and 17 cases of illegal transfer. Families have abandoned their plots either because of their decision to return to their home provinces or because the project is too far from their place of work (usually in Metro Manila). Many of the families who had transferred their plots illegally claimed to have resorted to selling their rights to others because of financial need. The NHA has adopted a policy of cancellation of allocation to abandonees and the repossession of sold plots. Families who have given up their home lot either by abandonment or illegal sale can no longer avail themselves of government assistance if they are found squatting again.

Formerly, the NHA policy on illegal occupancy, either by illegal purchase or by squatting, was to eject trespassing families (presumably by force if necessary) from the plots concerned. Subsequently, however, the NHA reviewed its policy and it is now possible for illegal occupation to be

Dasmariñas Bagong Bayan: established settlers. This family moved in one year before photograph was taken

Dasmariñas Bagong Bayan: about a year after resettlement, considerable house consolidation has taken place

regularized and for the occupants legally to purchase the plot they are occupying. Nevertheless, because the majority of such families are from higher income groups (presumably some are skilled or clerical employees of the on-site industrial operations), NHA asks them to pay 25 per cent more than the normally subsidized lease or ownership cost. Despite the premium they pay, families from lower middle and middle income groups still receive highly subsidized housing originally intended for low income families.

In implementing rules and regulations there is a need to strengthen the organization of the project to check these problems. This is especially so with illegal occupancy because project inspectors are often not able immediately to determine violations of regulations concerning occupancy.

(VIII) Financial Arrangements

At the start of the project in 1974, money for development was released through a presidential directive to the Ministry of the Budget upon submission of a work programme by the National Housing Authority.

Development and administration costs were incorporated in the NHA annual budget. Funds for physical development were included in the capital expenditures budget, funds for expropriation were incorporated under the land assembly programme, and funds for industrial/commercial estate development and livelihood components were included in the employment opportunities programme. The Project Team of Dasmariñas Bagong Bayan calculates the yearly budgetary requirement. This is assessed and approved by management and incorporated in the NHA annual budget.

Partial cost recovery was to be achieved in terms of the collection of amortization from resident beneficiaries. Selling prices of disposable lots have been fixed with the cost of residential lots cross subsidized by the commercial/ industrial components. All other items are considered to be direct expenditures of the authority (in effect, therefore, the project does substantially subsidize participants).

A billing and collection system was designed to achieve cost recovery. However, to date it has not proved very successful. In October 1981, the project had a default rate of 40 per cent. To attain a better performance record, the project management believes that the economic development of the residents must be improved.

To this end the NHA has initiated a Livelihood Development Programme. This programme organizes loans for families to enable them to set up small businesses. It also provides occupational training and arranges job placements. Another activity has involved arranging for exporters to deliver simple process work to households, which is paid for at piece rates when the companies collect the finished items. More than 800 families have been assisted through such programmes to date.

Chapter 7

Summing Up: The Future of Sites and Services as a Low Income Housing Strategy

7.1 Trends Discernible from the Reviewed Seminar Projects

Virtually all the schemes characterize a movement away from conventional housing which is generally costly and an inappropriate answer to low income housing demand in terms of space as well as of physical forms. In such conventional housing schemes, costs were generally only partially passed on to the residents, cushioning them from severe financial strain, but resulting in huge unrecoverable government outlays and an insufficient number of units, often in the wrong places. The schemes reviewed provide plots and basic shelter at lower cost and with more flexibility to match residents' demands.

However, in most cases the sites and services schemes reviewed can be judged as only the first step in the right direction. Generally, infrastructure standards are still too high, and in virtually all schemes there is a tendency to build more on-plot than would be desirable, if it is reasonable to assume that this aspect of housing is generally handled better by the residents than by government agencies. This assumption, in fact, is vindicated in all schemes where residents have already been in occupation for some time. Experiences in Arumbakkam (Madras), Dagat-Dagatan (Manila), and Simomulyo (Surabaya), for example, have shown that good, functional housing, appropriate to the people's needs, will be arranged by the residents themselves within a supportive environment created by government. In schemes where core units provided by government were perceived as obstructive rather than supportive, such core units were (partially) torn down or adapted by the residents upon occupation of the plots. This, obviously, is a waste of scarce resources.

In cities where several schemes have been implemented over time, generally a gradual improvement is discernible along the above dimensions: infrastructure standards are lowered and on-plot development is reduced. This is particularly discernible in Manila and Bangkok, and it shows that housing agencies are gradually coming to terms with these essential elements of the sites and services strategy.

Obviously, this has a cost reducing influence on the scheme: lower standards of infrastructure are cheaper to construct (and also to maintain if the quality

142

of infrastructural work is not affected, but only the degree) and so are housing units with a low core housing contents.

A related financial issue is the extent of subsidy incorporated in the schemes. While initially full cost recovery was attempted, there is now a clearly discernible trend not to include trunk infrastructure costs in recoverable costs. Obviously, it would be unreasonable to include such infrastructure costs fully if trunk infrastructure serves wider areas than just the project. In principle such costs could be apportioned, but apparently agencies find it easier not to include them at all in recoverable project costs but rather to treat them as city-wide overheads recoverable through local rates or taxation. On equity grounds the case for such an approach is strong: the government is seen to treat all neighbourhoods on a par.

Another area where subsidies seem to be irrepressible is the pricing of project land. In most of the reviewed schemes, project land was not priced at market value. In many cases the land concerned was government land to begin with or was acquired many years prior to the project's implementation. Generally, no reassessment of land values was carried out at the time of implementation. A subsidy on the land price is highly recommendable if subsidy levels are sustainable on a large scale and if such subsidies are part of a well-planned land disposal policy. This, unfortunately, was not the case in most schemes. Consequently, land subsidies tend to be *ad hoc*, contributing to distortions in the urban land market.

In most schemes client participation is low (although some changes were discernible in cities where more projects were carried out over time, notably Madras and Manila). This is most acute in the project identification and preparation stages. Generally, marketability of the plot is assumed rather than tested. Of course, in a suppliers' market like the urban low income housing market, such an assumption is not incorrect, but surely schemes would have been tailored to client demand if more market research had been carried out among the client groups prior to planning. This is not difficult to do: surveys in slum areas asking people about their willingness to pay for various housing options in terms of location, plot size, and core house types may not be completely reliable, but they will certainly lead to better planning than having no data at all. In implementation, too, participation is limited. Infrastructure and housing plots are generally developed exclusively by government agencies. Even in the obviously participatory stage of home extension the creative energy of residents is usually not fully utilized. Strict project rules in this regard lead to less than optimal utilization of people's resources.

7.2 Confronting the Constraints

An overriding constraint visible in almost all projects consists of the internal organizational structure of the implementing agencies. There are generally characterized by relatively rigid administrative rules and procedures. This often also affects the working relationship with other agencies providing inputs for the project. These factors may well prove to be the most serious obstacles to housing progress in future. Conventional housing as a strategy was not very successful for reasons inherent in the type of housing projects, but also because institutional problems prevented the delivery of large numbers of units. Changing from one type of project to another was necessary, but not sufficient to achieve a greater deal of success in the housing field. In fact, institutional problems are likely to be more confounding in sites and services projects than in conventional projects. First, housing professionals are not yet so conversant with such projects; secondly, a larger number of agencies are generally involved, requiring more emphasis on interagency coordination; and finally, client participation, which is an integral element in sites and services schemes, requires a flexible response from implementing agencies.

Institutional problems are rooted in attitudes and vested interests (see Wegelin, 1982b). Inflexible attitudes are the result of conventional practices in professional education, particularly architecture and engineering. This situation is slowly changing; there is now a growing awareness that trained professionals should play a supporting rather than a directing role in schemes like sites and services. Vested interests will be much more difficult to overcome. Sites and services projects are not very attractive to housing professionals: contracts are generally smaller (resulting in lower official and unofficial earnings) than in conventional housing and more difficult to carry out. The phasing of contracts is very desirable (because residents can move in earlier), but it compounds such difficulties. Another real threat to architects and engineers is that the demand for their services is comparatively low in sites and services projects, whereas such projects will generate increasing demands for managerial, financial, and social skills. As architectural and engineering skills are generally scarce, this could be a welcome development leading to a larger number of projects being developed, provided the additional non-technical matching skills are added in sufficient quantity and provided administrative routines can be made more flexible and functional.

Clearly, then, the sites and services approach is more demanding of the concerned agencies in terms of specialized manpower resources. More complex research inputs are required along with more specialized support systems to enable the implementation of projects, subsequent housing and community development and payment collection to proceed satisfactorily. The costs involved in recruiting and developing such vital personnel are likely to be felt as a considerable burden on these relatively pioneering projects. In future, however, as more and more experience is gained, these costs, along with costs resulting from mistakes, will decline, thus enhancing the efficiency of these components.

In any event, there are positive signs from some of the implementing agencies of the development of both more appropriate structures and suitably trained and committed staff. The main agencies implementing Arumbakkam, Vashi, and Dakshinpuri resettlement projects are clearly developing more effective organizations and more experienced staff who are more attuned to the complex challenge of sites and services project management. Also the National Housing Authorities of Thailand and the Philippines have displayed a willingness to learn from earlier project mistakes. This willingness to learn has resulted in the modification of project management teams and closer attention to planning goals and their realization. In addition, specialized training programmes for agency staff and the growing exchange of information on project experiences are helping to gear up these organizations to the sites and services task.

In cities where slum upgrading programmes are being implemented alongside sites and services, such specialized staff can maximize their efficiency by scheduling their involvement in both activities. Clearly, many advantages could accrue from this, not only in terms of the efficient use of scarce specialized manpower but also in terms of coordination and feedback between the complementary strategies of slum upgrading and sites and services. One such advantage would be the possibility of identifying participants for future or current sites and services projects and recruiting them, thus enabling greater participation by sites and services clients in the design of their communities.

An additional constraint is the availability of suitable land. The questions of economic, efficient, and non-subsidized land utilization, the long-term availability of land, and locational issues are interrelated and pose serious dilemmas to the sites and services approach. Among the reviewed projects, seven utilized land that belonged to government departments or enterprises, and in three other cases it was expropriated for the purpose. Only in the remaining four projects was the land purchased in the market, presumably at prevailing prices. It is likely that in many of the countries concerned, where elite interests are firmly entrenched, access to land for sites and services will dry up once government land resources have been used up.

As cities grow, mechanisms must be developed to reserve suitable land for low income housing purposes. Land banking deserves wider application in this regard, whereas no alternative option may be found in developing smaller sites. Such sites are often closer to city centres than most project areas discussed at the seminar. This will make them more expensive in terms of land costs, but these may be offset by reduced costs of infrastructure provision and transportation to work (see National Housing Authority of Thailand, 1980). However, the land market in most cities is fraught with market imperfections. Some of these are inherent in the nature of the land market, but land speculation and irrational management of government land contribute to this. Government intervention in the private land market is generally politically difficult or financially disastrous.

In Indian cities the political will and legal mechanisms to expropriate land are strong and the application and development of sites and services projects can be expected to continue but in South East Asian cities, notably in the Philippines, Thailand, and Indonesia, the future of sites and services looks more grim. Land pricing in the highly speculative land markets in urban areas in these countries prohibits any extensive exploration of utilizing central city locations for sites and services projects. (The Dagat-Dagatan project can be seen as an exceptional case that was largely dependent on the highly political factors surrounding the Tondo Foreshore redevelopment. It is unlikely that another project of this scale will be mooted in the central areas of Metro Manila.) This implies that if sites and services projects are to continue into future decades in these countries, locations will become more remote from city centres, less relevant to the lower income target groups, and gradually less attractive to even those families from the higher percentiles of the low income groups because of higher costs incurred in resettling, the social costs of dislocation, and the increases in travel time.

7.3 The Role of Sites and Services Projects in Future Low Income Housing Strategies

First of all, it should be noted that sites and services cannot be considered the last word in low income housing strategies even now. As noted in earlier chapters, it is generally regarded as a complementary strategy to slum upgrading. In fact, slum upgrading is more attractive to low income families than sites and services in a number of aspects: it is cheaper, and there is no dislocation from living areas, places of work and schools. It reasserts the rights of the poor to live in their city instead of being pushed out. It reaches very low income people in its environmental and socio-economic upgrading. However, in many cases it does not offer security of tenure and often its environmental upgrading forms only a marginal improvement on existing conditions. Sites and services, in contrast, does offer security of tenure and a substantial improvement in housing and environmental conditions. However, it caters for a different segment of housing demand: generally those who are slightly less poor and for whom it is not absolutely disastrous to move. As such it is rightfully complementary to slum upgrading.

Another important point to note is that within the broad term 'sites and services', there are many variations on the theme. The schemes reviewed in this book testify to this. Some schemes rely on the city for many things, e.g. employment, trunk infrastructure, but are otherwise fairly large (Arumbakkam, Madras, and Metroville, Karachi). Some are a self-contained new town (Dasmarinas, Philippines, and Bang Plee Bang Bor, Thailand) or a fraction of it (Vashi, New Bombay). The extent of 'core housing' varies enormously from the complete base houses in the Perumnas projects in Bekasi and Medan, Indonesia, to the vacant plot development in Dakshinpuri, Delhi.

This range of options across a wide spectrum is likely to widen in future. More and more agencies are coming to realize that each individual situation demands its own approach. Thus we see hybrids of slum upgrading and sites and services appearing. Hannamula Camp and Summitpura, Colombo, Sri Lanka, are completely different project examples of hybrids within the same metropolitan area. Slum reconstruction as practised in Habitat Hyderabad,

India, is yet another totally different example, and so is the Building Together approach in Bangkok, Thailand.

Yet within this spectrum, there will continue to be a need for new, cheap, secure and suitably located, serviced housing plots, as long as the demand on the urban low income housing market grows (and there is very little likelihood that this will not happen). However, the efficient application of such projects, incorporating the development, as noted in the previous section, of smaller, more centrally located areas, will require considerably more flexibility on the part of implementing agencies than has been displayed so far. Apart from the need to avoid the more obvious mistakes (such as, for example, an inability to provide bulk water supply as in Metroville, Karachi), this will entail a willingness to explore more client-oriented approaches; i.e. to tailor projects more to target group demands. Areas of crucial interest are likely to be proximity to work and socio-economic support schemes, rather than the physical dimensions of the schemes, although the need to reduce standards and costs remains for infrastructure provision. By the same token, on-plot development by the agency should be minimal, at most comprising a sanitary core.

In order to be able to develop more client-oriented approaches, agencies will find maximum community participation indispensable, no matter how troublesome and time consuming this may be at times. Such developments will also have staffing consequences for implementing agencies. The gradual process of developing effective and appropriate housing agencies depends largely on creating responsible and cooperative interaction between the agency personnel and the community. Units dealing with sites and services projects along the above dimensions will increasingly come to be staffed by professionals with a social work or community development background. This is a necessary step if the sites and services approach is to become a significant mechanism in providing basic community services, public utilities, and shelter at comparatively low costs.

However, even if implementing agencies develop in that direction, it is unlikely that sites and services projects will play a quantitatively important role in future, unless urban land policies undergo significant changes. As long as land speculation and land withholding continues unchecked, it will become increasingly difficult to acquire sites which are both cheap and sufficiently accessible to employment opportunities to enable a meaningful contribution to be made to the shelter problems of the urban poor.

References

Churchill Anthony A. (1980), *Shelter*, Poverty and Basic Needs Series, IBRD, Washington DC.

Housing and Urban Development Corporation (1978), *Shelter*, New Delhi.

International Bank for Reconstruction and Development (1974), *'Sites and Services Projects'*, Washington DC.

National Housing Authority of Thailand (1980). *'Present Standards and Prices in the Housing Market in Bangkok'*, Bangkok.

Rodell, M. J. (1981). 'A note on African sites and services programmes', paper presented at the seminar on 'Sites and Services: Exploring the Asian Experience', Bangkok.

Sarin, Madhu (1982). 'The rich, the poor and the land question', paper presented at the seminar on 'Land for Housing the Poor: Towards Positive Action in Asian Cities', Bangkok (to be published in the forthcoming book with the same title edited by S. Angel, R. J. Archer, S. Tanphiphat, and E. A. Wegelin).

Siddiqui, Islamuddin (1980), 'The implementation of the Metroville I project in Karachi', working paper no.2, Human Settlements Division, Asian Institute of Technology, Bangkok.

Wegelin, Emiel A. (1978), *'Low-income Housing and Development: A Case Study in Peninsular Malaysia'*, Boston/Leiden.

Wegelin, Emiel A. (1982), 'The economics of land tenure regularization in Katchi Abadi improvement', in J. J. van der Linden and Yap Kioe Sheng (eds), *'Between Bastidwellers and Bureaucrats: Lessons of Squatter Upgrading in Karachi'*, Amsterdam.

Wegelin, Emiel A. (1983), 'From building to enabling housing strategies in Asia: Institutional problems', in M. J. Rodell and Reinhard Skinner, *Essays on Self-help Housing Policies*, London.

Index